great SETS

7 ROADMAPS TO SPECTACULAR QUILTS

SHARYN CRAIG

C&T PUBLISHING INC.

PUBLISHER Amy Marson
EDITORIAL DIRECTOR Gailen Runge
EDITOR Pamela Mostek
TECHNICAL EDITORS Carolyn Aune, Joyce Engels Lytle
COPYEDITOR/PROOFREADER Eva Simoni Erb
COVER DESIGNER Kristin Yenche
BOOK DESIGNER Staci Harpole, Cubic Design
DESIGN DIRECTOR Diane Pedersen
ILLUSTRATOR Kirstie L. McCormick
PRODUCTION ASSISTANT Luke Mulks
PHOTOGRAPHY Carina Woolrich
COVER PHOTOGRAPHER Sharon Risedorph

Published by C&T Publishing, Inc., P.O. Box 1456, Lafayette, California, 94549

Front cover: *Adam's Quilt*
Back cover: *Follow His Star, Make Mine Pastel*

Library of Congress Cataloging-in-Publication Data
Craig, Sharyn Squier.
Great sets : 7 roadmaps to spectacular quilts / Sharyn Craig.
p. cm.
Includes index.
ISBN 1-57120-224-2 (Paper trade)
1. Patchwork quilts–Design. 2. Quilting. 3. Patchwork. I. Title.
TT835.C73314 2004
746.46–dc22
2003017418

Printed in China
10 9 8 7 6 5 4 3 2 1

Dedication

I dedicate this book to my grandchildren, Ashlyn and Adam Craig. Through their eyes I experience new and fresh ideas. Through their unconditional love I greet each new day with peace and anticipation.

Acknowledgments

I wish I could personally name and thank each quilter who made a block for the quilts in this book. I hope all of you recognize your blocks.

I wish I could personally name each student in every class I've ever taught who inspired me to look for more answers and more solutions.

I wish I could personally name each individual whose quilts were printed in magazines and books or were hung in various quilt shows around the country that I've seen. Those quilts inspired me.

Without all these unnamed quilters I doubt that I would have been able to sit here today sharing these ideas and quilts with you. To each of these individuals, I say thank you.

I can name the individuals who created quilts by filling their blocks into my overall designs. These quiltmakers include Carolyn Smith, Margret Reap, Laurine Leeke, Sandy Andersen, Ruth Gordy, Marnie Santos, Irene Mueller, Joann Stuebing, Shelley Knapp, Pat Marean, Louise Hixon, Mary Pavlovich, Sally Collins, Sandra Munsey, Linda Packer, Lynn Johnson, and Connie Chunn. These quilters went that extra mile. They helped me work through the problems so I could share answers with you. They made the quilts that you'll see in these pages. These same quilts will inspire you and give you answers. "Thank you" hardly seems like enough, but I mean it with all my heart.

You'll see some blocks in these quilts that were started in workshops taught by professional quilt teachers. You may see a block in a quilt that was inspired by an ad in a magazine. It was never my intention to claim any of these blocks as my own inventions. In many cases I assigned a name to the block because I didn't know of any other name it might already have. If I failed to give proper credit to any particular quiltmaker or block designer, please know that it was not intentional. Giving proper credit is important in our industry, but so often we really don't know whom to acknowledge.

I would also like to acknowledge the time that my friend Stevii Graves spent reading over the manuscript for comprehension and clarity. They say that when you need a job done, ask a busy person. Well I did, and she said yes. Thank you, Stevii.

Another thank you to Moda Fabrics for the continued generosity they've shown in providing fabric for so many of the quilts you'll see throughout the book. Just when I wondered what color I should work with this time, a packet of fabric arrived. How fun to find that kind of inspiration just when I needed it.

I also need to acknowledge my family for all their support, love, and understanding. I most especially need to thank my husband George, who listened, proofed, viewed quilts, cleaned house, did dishes, and sat alone many evenings and weekends watching television, while I was on the computer or in my sewing room working on the book. I love you, hon.

Table of Contents

Introduction

y book *Setting Solutions* was all about helping you get your blocks into a finished quilt top. You'll find even more great ideas for doing just that in this, my next book, *Great Sets*. One of my goals in writing this book was to show you the power of the setting when you create your quilts. In fact, it can be even more important than the blocks you use in that setting. You'll see that many of the quilts in this book are even made with the same blue and ecru Sawtooth Star blocks. Each of these quilts takes on its own unique personality depending on the set that the quiltmaker used.

We learn by doing, so let's jump in and see what great ideas are ahead. In Chapter One you'll find some good, solid information necessary to understanding the rest of the chapters. I'll briefly talk about how to approach the problem of size reconciliation. If you want more information than you find in this book, I refer you to my previous book, *Setting Solutions*, where I go into greater detail about the problem of size differential and how to resolve the discrepancies.

I'll also give you a unique approach to working with color in a totally different way. Over and over again I hear, "I need help with color." Well, here you have "The Paper Bag Game." What does that mean, you're wondering? You'll have to read Chapter One to find out.

In this book I'm proposing that you start from the "outside" and plug your blocks into the basic equation... that's one thing that makes this book unique. I present what I call Setting Maps, a concept I introduced in *Setting Solutions*, only in that book I called them Project Maps. In Chapter 1 you'll get a glimpse of all seven maps. Then in Chapters 2 through 8, I'll elaborate on these seven settings.

I also provide the simple math concepts you need to take your blocks of any size and plug them into the maps found in each of the chapters, along with variations or "What Ifs" for each of the maps. Perhaps after reading through the book and studying the quilts, you'll be able to come up with some "What Ifs" and variations of your own.

Chapter 9 is a gallery of quilts that were inspired by, but didn't exactly follow, a given map. Hopefully you'll be inspired to come up with more new ideas from studying these photos, as well as all of the photos in the specific chapters.

For those of you who may not have odd blocks lying around, I haven't forgotten you! Or perhaps some of you would rather start from scratch to use these Setting Maps. In either case you'll find block patterns in Chapter 10 so you can make blocks, many of which are featured in one or more of the quilts throughout the book. Now I don't want to hear any excuses about why you can't have fun and play with the concepts in this book just because you don't have blocks to use!

Chapter 10 is also full of other useful information. You'll find charts—lots and lots of charts. Throughout the book I'll be referring to these charts, so I suggest looking them over before you begin a project.

Throughout the book I've also included quotes from "real life" quiltmakers who have used the Setting Maps to create their own quilts, and were pleased to add their comments and reactions to encourage all of you to give the process a try, too. Thanks to all of them for enthusiastically sharing.

You won't find the exact recipe for making any one quilt in this book. There are no yardage amounts, no exact number of pieces you would need to cut, no finished sizes for your quilts. If you are a new quilter and need more information about how to get started, then I refer you to the book I co-authored with Harriet Hargrave, *The Art of Classic Quiltmaking*. It is a great encyclopedic, reference-style book, with a lot of useful information.

So, now it's time to get started. First, read Chapter 1, which gives you an overview of the seven setting options. Then look through all the rest of the chapters. Next, get out some blocks and see what develops!

Sharyn

Understanding the Basics

"Nothing
makes the point
stronger than
actually seeing
examples."

SHARYN

Understanding the Basics

The first thing I'm going to do is introduce you to the Setting Maps for each of the seven sets featured in this book. The shaded area on each Map represents your individual focus blocks.

Shaded area = focus block.

These are just simplified mini maps, so you and I can be on the same wavelength as we begin. You will find more information about each setting in its own specific chapter, plus photographs of quilts to go along with the information. Nothing makes the point stronger than actually seeing examples.

Two-for-One Set   Windblown-Square Set

Square-in-a-Square Set   Chain Set   Crossover Set

Garden-Maze Set   Ring-Around-the-Block Set

Frequently, when making a quilt you are following a pattern. Someone has predetermined exactly how many blocks you are making, what size the quilt is going to be, what setting you are using, and even what the borders are going to be. This is the "paint-by-numbers" approach to making a quilt. When we first start quilting, those specific recipes can be really helpful.

The longer we quilt, however, the more we find the pre-determined recipe doesn't always fit our needs. Perhaps you thought the recipe would work when you started the blocks, but the further you got into the quilt, the more dissatisfied you became. So the project sits there unfinished. Lots of quilters have UFOs (Un-Finished Objects), or blocks, not sewn into a quilt.

Maybe you made the blocks, won them at guild, inherited them from someone, or bought them at a flea market. No one is around to tell you how to set those blocks. So what do you do with them? This can be a puzzle. The most common solution is to set them straight with simple sashing and cornerstones. You might get really adventurous and put the blocks on point with sashing and cornerstones.

After reading this book you will no longer have to choose the obvious. You will have seven new, totally different answers to that dilemma. The seven Setting Maps in this book provide you with lots of great material for finishing up all of those UFOs.

Before we go any further, I realize that there are some of you who don't have unfinished blocks tucked away in your sewing rooms. Or maybe you prefer to start from scratch and make new blocks. If that's the case, check out Chapter 10 where I've included block patterns so you can do just that. Then you'll be ready to decide which Setting Map to use to complete your quilt.

For the rest of you, if you haven't already gotten those UFOs out of hiding, it's time to do it now! How many UFOs do you have? If you have a lot, you might want to select just one set of blocks to begin with, perhaps the one that you like the most. Or maybe you should choose the one with the most blocks. It really doesn't matter what blocks you pick first. You don't even have to stay with that choice. As you get into the information in this chapter, if you decide to change your mind, go for it. But it does help to have a particular set of blocks in mind when you work through some of this material.

Once you've made a selection about which set of blocks to work with, take a few minutes to fill out the following worksheet. If the blocks are all different sizes, write the sizes down. Not all questions need to have an answer, but if there is an answer, write it down. Keep this worksheet with the blocks. Making good notes at this point will save you a lot of time in the long run.

Size Reconciliation

Size differential is, without a doubt, the biggest problem most quilters face when they have a set of blocks and want to set them into a quilt. These differences can occur when one quiltmaker sews all the blocks or when lots of different people make the blocks. It doesn't matter how or why it happens, we just want to fix that problem.

There are three basic ways to reconcile size differential:
- Remake the blocks.
- Trim down the blocks to make them all the same size.
- Add to the blocks in the form of framing strips or triangles.

Setting Worksheet

How many blocks do you have?

What size are they?

Do they need to sit on point or straight, or does orientation matter?

What color, or colors, are they?

Do you like the colors?

Do you want to stay with those colors in your final quilt, or would you rather change that feature?

Do you know how big a quilt you want to make?

What do you like or dislike about the blocks?

Remake the Block

Remaking the block doesn't sound like much fun, and it usually isn't. It means carefully picking apart each and every seam, checking each piece to make sure it was cut accurately in the beginning, then stitching the pieces back together. This is the method of last choice for most quilters, but it is an option.

Trim Down the Blocks

When most quilters hear, "trim down the blocks," they immediately react, "That can't work, I'll lose points." That may be true, and if it would bother you, then you would probably not choose this option. But, before ruling this method out, look at your blocks. Not all blocks have points to begin with, either because the design doesn't have points, or because faulty construction already eliminated points. In those instances, do you really think it's going to hurt the final quilt if you trim a little more away? Study the quilts in this book to see how little negative visual impact trimming the blocks really has on the finished quilt.

Add to the Blocks

Since adding to the blocks allows me to cope with the problem of size differences, I think of these add-on pieces as coping triangles and coping strips. When using coping pieces I always make the coping pieces larger than needed, then trim. I frame the largest blocks first to determine what size pieces I will need to add to the smaller blocks.

Coping pieces can present visually in one of three ways: Negative, Accent, or Power. What do each of these terms imply?

Negative. You can't see it. The coping pieces become invisible when the added fabric matches either the block background or the background next to it, or when the coping pieces become a part of the Setting Map, or setting structure. This last statement will make more sense as you read the rest of the book and study the quilts. Settings like the Garden Maze are constructed with framing strips for each block first. Because of the way you color the

entire quilt, that coping strip becomes part of the structure of the set and can be invisible as a tool used to reconcile size.

Accent. You can see the coping pieces, but they don't overwhelm the blocks. You select accent colors to enhance the blocks, not to totally change them. Accent strips and triangles work with the block to help create the color scheme, but not to override the colors in the original blocks.

Power. Just like it implies, select strong colors for the coping pieces to negate the colors of the original blocks. Power pieces are used when you don't like the original colors or if you just don't want to see those colors.

Color

Nobody needs help with pure color. There, I've said it. You may not believe it, but it is true. All colors go together. That doesn't mean you like all colors, but they do go together. If you don't like a particular color combination, then you shouldn't use those colors together. Your goal in making a quilt should be to like what you make. You don't need to please the rest of the world, just please yourself! That takes a lot of confidence, but it is something we each need to strive toward. Meanwhile, while working on building that confidence, let's have some fun and play with color in a new way. There is no magic color formula. It is a skill gained through practice. That means you have to jump in and take chances.

I made the statement that all colors go together. Make a list of some of the color schemes that you like. I'll start the process. You don't have to work with my list, but it is a place to start. Add to this list, or eliminate ones you don't like.

Red, white, and blue	Red and black
Pink and green	Green and blue
Yellow, green, and blue	Purple and pink
Purple and teal	Pink, orange, and yellow
Red and green	On and on and on.

Then there are also the adjectives that make you think of certain colors: pastel, tropical, Oriental, child-like, graphic, homespun, country, Southwest, autumn, patriotic, '30s...are you getting the idea?

Sometimes I automatically know, without a doubt, what kinds of colors I want to work with when I get out my blocks. *The Patriotic Games* on page 74 is one such example. I could have opted to lose the red, white, and blue, but I didn't. I decided to warm up the blocks by adding lots of that gold-ish color, but I stayed patriotic from beginning to end by using lots more reds and blues.

Baby Dresdens on page 38 is another example of knowing just what I wanted. When the pastel Dresden Plate blocks were on the wall, I knew I wanted to make a soft, spring-like quilt, so I pulled soft pastel floral prints to keep that feeling.

Other times I'm looking at blocks on the wall and I have no idea what direction to take. When you look at the basic blue Sawtooth Star blocks, for example, you will see safe, sweet, ordinary blue and ecru blocks.

Basic Blue Sawtooth Star blocks

The Paper Bag Approach

I know lots of colors "work" with blue, but as I look at these blocks, I realize that I have nothing particular in mind for this quilt, so what colors should I use? What direction should I take?

When it makes no difference at all, it can be very overwhelming. But that's when I really have fun. I make a list of colors and adjectives and write each of them on a separate piece of paper. I put the slips into a brown paper bag, close my eyes, and draw a slip of paper from the bag. That's it. That's the color scheme for the blue stars.

" I loved the 'paper bag' approach to choosing color and deciding which setting to use. What an easy way to make a difficult decision. Using this method helps jump-start your brain! "

Margret Reap, El Cajon, California

I never write anything on the slip of paper that I wouldn't be willing to work with. I do, however, allow myself to change my recipe plan as the quilt develops.

An example of this could be that I pull out a slip that says "blue and yellow." As I start pulling fabric to work with, I decide to audition some green with the palette. Next I try a little peach. Oh, what about lavender? Next thing you know, I have gone from a blue and yellow quilt to a more generalized pastel recipe. Remember, I'm writing the rules, so I can change them whenever I want. It is, however, a fun and different way to start. It gives you the focus you need to move forward when you don't have a clue what direction you want to go.

At times I treat these color exercises as Discipline Challenges. If I write monochromatic on the slip of paper, then my challenge is to stay within the blue to white color scheme. My favorite palette is very scrappy—the more colors and the more fabrics the better. If I am forced to limit my choices, I am definitely going to learn and grow as a quiltmaker. It's too easy to always make safe, predictable quilts.

The Oncall Quilters

When I'm working on a new concept or need help making blocks or quilts, I count on my group of loyal quilters, the Oncall Quilters, who answer the call. When the Oncall Quilters began working with these blue star blocks, we each deliberately took a different color scheme and a different Setting Map. It's easy for me to say that the same blocks will work in different color schemes or different settings, but it's much more effective when you can see an example. We selected blue for our focus color because it's a very "quilter-friendly" color; however, we could have chosen any color to experiment with.

Analyzing Your Blocks

Let's get back to your blocks. You've decided which ones to use. You've written down some initial reactions to the colors. Are you staying with those comments, or do you want to modify them? Remember, you're the one in charge. Do you have a color scheme in mind for your blocks, or would you like to try the Paper Bag game? The words you write on the slips of paper can be actual color schemes, or they can be descriptive adjectives. Or you can write both on one slip of paper. Could you make a patriotic quilt in blue, green, and yellow? Why not give it at try?

Okay, you have your blocks and you've picked a color scheme. Next, start pulling fabric from your shelves—lots and lots of fabric. During this audition phase I really don't try to overanalyze any particular piece of fabric. I don't think about how many I need, or whether these "two" fabrics will look good together. I just pull fabric. I'm lucky. I have a huge stash of fabric, collected since 1978, to work with. If you're a new quilter and don't have that fabric on hand, then you may need to go to the quilt shop and start buying fabric.

Buying Fabric

How much fabric to buy? Next to "I need help with color," "How much fabric should I buy?" is the second most frequent question I'm asked. My usual answer is $1/3$ to $1/2$ yard of any one fabric. There are some fabrics, like background options or border pieces that I'll buy $1 1/2$ to 3 yards at a time. But for the most part, I find smaller pieces to be quite adequate.

One of the main reasons I like to work scrappy is because I never have to worry about running out of fabric. When you decide to make a three- or five-fabric quilt, then you have to be much more careful about yardage. With scrap, if I run out of one piece of fabric, I just substitute something else.

Choosing the Setting

Okay, you have your blocks. You've determined the color direction you are heading. Now what? Now you select one of the Settings. Look at the full Setting Maps with each chapter to get a better idea of the potential. You'll also want to spend some time studying the pictures in each chapter. The visual stimulation and inspiration of the pictures will be very helpful in making your selection.

The longer you work with this book and the concepts I'm presenting, the more you'll realize that it doesn't really matter if you begin with choosing color or picking the set. I've actually made some quilts where I started with the set in mind, discovered I had no blocks that I wanted to work with, and had to make blocks just so I could explore a particular setting.

Sampler Chain on page 50 is a prime example of one time I did just that. I wanted to show how successful the Chain Set could be for sampler blocks. I didn't have any sampler blocks on hand, so I had to make them first. I had all the block patterns in Chapter 10 to work with. In this instance, I picked the set, then determined the blocks, and finally selected the colors.

The bottom line is it doesn't matter where you begin the process. I think most of us start with color. That may be because you want to work with that new fabric you just purchased. For some of you color may be one of the most difficult parts of making a quilt, but it is also the first thing we notice about a quilt. Working with colors that make you comfortable and happy is definitely a catalyst to being inspired to work on a quilt.

If you ask your children what color quilt they want, and they select a color scheme you don't like, you're going to find working on that quilt to be very difficult. I do like to make quilts for my family, but I do not ask them what color they want. I make a quilt. If they like it and make noises like they would like to own it—assuming I'm willing to part with it— then fine. Meanwhile I've been able to work on a quilt that energizes me from start to finish.

" You have created a monster! I've just finished the fourth quilt using these techniques...and from blocks that have been just sitting in my sewing room collecting dust. Just call me Sharyn Craiglovich! "

Mary Pavlovich, Upland, California

Getting Started

If you have your blocks and have selected colors and fabric to work with, then it's time to read ahead. You can read and read and look at all the pictures over and over again, but eventually you must make a decision. If you don't, then those blocks are going to remain UFOs for a long time to come.

If you're still having trouble choosing between the various setting options, you might consider putting each of the choices on separate slips of paper and picking one of those out of a paper bag. Why not? If you're up for the new challenge and really want to get those blocks from the UFO stage to the finished quilt stage, then it's time to move forward. On that note, let's turn the page and keep reading.

Two-for-One Set

"This is a
great set for
almost any kind
of blocks,
whether they
are all the same
or each
is different."

SHARYN

Two-for-One Set

 first introduced you to the Two-for-One Set in *Setting Solutions*. The concept is quite simple. You frame some of the blocks with coping triangles and the alternating blocks with coping strips. When framing this way, you end up with some of your blocks sitting straight and others on point. This is a great set for almost any kind of blocks, whether they are all the same or each is different, as in the case of a sampler quilt. About the only time you wouldn't want to consider this set as a possibility would be if all your blocks need to orient straight or all on point.

Setting Variations

With this simple concept there are actually four different formats you could opt for, as illustrated in the following Setting Maps:

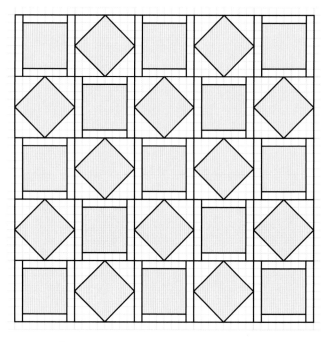

Two-for-One Set, straight, starting with coping strips

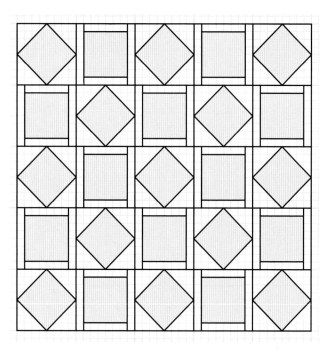

Two-for-One Set, straight, starting with coping triangles

Two-for-One Set, on point, starting with coping triangles

Two-for-One Set, on point, starting with coping strips

Because the framing pieces are "coping" strips and triangles, it's a great set to use when you need to reconcile size differences between your blocks. If you have a large size differential between blocks, you might want to consider additional coping strips prior to the actual framing. Sometimes these additional strips add spice and color to your blocks. You can use coping strips even when you don't need to fix size.

If you select one of the straight set variations, you will want to set an odd number of blocks in each direction to keep "balance." For instance, five rows with three blocks in each row, or seven rows with five blocks in each. If you were to use even numbers, like six rows with four blocks in each, the design would start with one frame and end with the other. The viewer tends to feel this is unfinished.

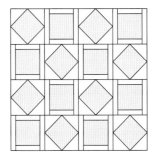

An even number of blocks set in a row creates a bad balance.

If you chose one of the diagonal settings, then you can use any number of blocks in either direction. If you look at the diagrams, you will see that in the diagonal version, all the outside blocks have either the coping triangles or the coping strips.

Where to Start

I usually have a plan when I start putting the blocks on the wall. This plan determines only whether I think I'm going to do the straight set or the diagonal set. I seldom stick to that plan, but it gives me a starting place. At this point it doesn't matter which frame (strip or triangle) is in the corner, just whether I plan a straight or diagonal finish. Some of this decision is based on how many blocks I have to work with.

Sometimes I'm thinking about the overall final size of the quilt as I make this determination. The diagonal set will make the quilt larger with fewer blocks. If I know I want a rectangle instead of a square, then I usually opt for the diagonal set, strictly because the straight set, which uses an odd number of blocks in each direction, tends to make either long skinny quilts, or very large ones.

Color and Basic Recipe

Next I select color and determine a basic recipe. By that I mean scrappy versus controlled. I could choose red and white and only plan two fabrics, or I could choose red and white but want to use dozens of fabrics. I think about which colors are going to be the strip frames and which are going to be the triangle frames. I like to audition the fabrics on the wall beside the blocks.

Sizing the Blocks

In working with this set, start by framing with the coping triangles. Chapter 10 works through the math involved for calculating the size of these triangles. It also gives you a chart of sizes to cut for a variety of different block sizes. The calculations and the chart allow for the straight of grain on the outside edge of the framed block. The math and the chart in Chapter 10 assumes that your blocks are all the same size. If your blocks are different sizes, I use the approach below.

 Cut 2 squares the same size as the largest focus block and cut the squares once corner to corner.

Cut squares diagonally.

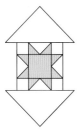 Attach the triangles to the largest block you're framing. Iron well.

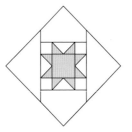

Attaching triangles to the block

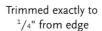 Trim to square up the block using a square rotary ruler. When squaring up the block, make sure to leave $1/4$" beyond the points of the original block to allow for the seam allowance. This is the size you will be making all the rest of the blocks.

 Cut more coping triangles the same size as in Step 1 and add them to your remaining blocks. Trim all the blocks to the same size.

| Trimmed exactly to $1/4$" from edge | Trimmed with lots of triangle remaining |

Example: The block is $9\,1/2$"(raw edge to raw edge).

Cut two $9\,1/2$" squares and cut diagonally in half to make the coping triangles. Add the triangles to the block.

Trim the completed block to size.

Coping triangles made this way are going to be very oversized, but very forgiving. Some quilters find that working with squares this large is too wasteful, but it does have the advantage of working on virtually all the blocks you are going to be re-sizing. That is assuming the size differential is within reasonable limits. If you are trying to treat a 4" block and a 12" block with the same coping triangles, it won't work. But an 11" block and a 12" block will work with these same triangles.

Adding the Strip Frames

Once you've determined the new-sized blocks you have from the triangle-framed units, you're ready to do the strip-framed blocks.

1 Determine the finished size of the original blocks and the finished size of the framed blocks. (The finished size is $1/2$" less than the cut size.)

Original block   Framed block

Cut size: black lines
Finished size: red lines

2 Subtract the finished size of the original block from the finished size of the triangle-framed block.

3 To find the finished width of the coping strips, divide your answer from Step 2 in half.

4 To determine the cut widths of the coping strips, add $1/2$" to your answer from Step 3. Then I like to pad that number by adding another $1/2$". Cut as many strips as you will need to frame the blocks. *Note: You do not have to calculate the exact length of the coping strips since they will be trimmed to size as they are sewn to the block.*

5 Sew the strips onto the block, adding strips to opposite sides of the block and trimming the length to the same size as the block. Add the remaining 2 strips in the same way.

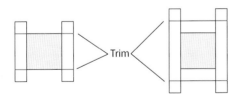

Trim

6 Iron the block well, and trim to the same size as the triangle-framed block. I'd rather cut away a little bit and make sure all the blocks are the same size and perfectly square.
Example: The original blocks are 9" finished.

Square up the triangle-framed 9" blocks to $13^1/2$" (raw edge to raw edge) so the finished block is then 13".

$$13" - 9" = 4"$$

$4" \div 2 = 2" + 1/2"$ (seam allowance) $+ 1/2"$ (pad factor) $= 3"$-wide strips to cut for framing the alternating blocks.

The newly framed block will measure 14". Trim to $13^1/2$" to match the triangle-framed blocks.

 TIP: *It makes no difference in what order you attach the strips to the block. Some like to sew opposing sides first, then the other two sides. Unless you are going for some sort of special effect color-wise, I wouldn't bother with mitering corners. If you do need to miter the corners for effect, you can still use oversized strips and trim the block afterwards.*

More Ideas

You don't have to stick to one of these four simple layouts. Try adding piecing to the coping triangles or coping strips. Or what if you put sashing between the blocks, simple or pieced? If you've never used this type of setting, I think you'll find that it is simple and fun. Plus, it has the potential of making a quilt look much more complicated than it actually is.

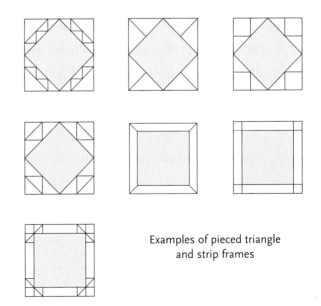

Examples of pieced triangle
and strip frames

Now let's look at some quilts created with this set. You can also check out additional quilts using this setting in Chapter 9, the gallery of this book.

Tropical Paradise

by Pat Marean, machine quilted by Phyllis Reddish, 56" x 84", 2002

This is an example of a straight set Two-for-One quilt that starts and ends with the triangle frame. Pat played carefully with the triangle framing pieces to create the secondary star in the center of the quilt. The strip frame on the central block is a darker blue than on the other blocks. The reason for that change was to make the frame blend into the framing triangles to better emphasize the star pattern.

Five Patch Sampler

by Sally Collins, 15 $^{1}/_{4}$" x 15 $^{1}/_{4}$", 2002

Sally's workmanship and color skills are amazing to me. The fact that she works in miniature makes them even more impressive. She made these nine little blocks as samples for a workshop she was teaching. She didn't want to make any more of the blocks but wanted a setting that would really showcase them. She came across the Two-for-One set in *Setting Solutions* and knew she had found the answer.

It's All in the Setting

by Carolyn Smith and Sharyn Craig, quilted by
Carolyn Smith, 44" x 56", 2002

Carolyn made the little 6" star blocks
years ago and gave them to me to
play with. I knew I wanted a simple
Two-for-One Set, but what about color?
I decided to use as many colors as
I could in framing these blocks. I
selected jewel tones for the framing
triangles and put the newly framed
blocks on point. I also pieced the side
and corner setting triangles rather
than using solid fabric. It added a little
more time to creating the quilt, but
what a difference it made to
the final outcome.

Stars Over Provence

by Carolyn Smith, 70" x 70", 2002

Here are some more of our basic
blue star blocks. First Carolyn set each
star block into a pieced triangle
frame. Her newly framed blocks are
8½" finished blocks. She set them into
a diagonal Two-for-One Set, starting
with the strip-framed pieces. Her color
scheme of blue and yellow really
livens up the blocks.

*"I must confess that I had an 'I
can't do that as well as Sharyn'
attitude until recently. The difference
is that I finally understand the
concept of choosing the setting and
color first—then making the blocks
fit. It really is so much easier."*

Carolyn Smith, El Cajon, California

Born Again

by Sharyn Craig, machine quilted by Shelley Knapp, 53" x 67", 2002

Here is another set of the basic blue blocks. My color assignment was red, black, and light blue. I framed each block with a narrow red strip first, primarily for a color accent, but it also helped to reconcile the sizes. I used black for the strip-framed blocks and light blue for the triangle frames. Once the finished blocks were on the wall I was bothered by how "flat" they appeared. I used the Corner Cutter technique described in Chapter 10 to attach new green and blue triangles, which really perked up the palette.

Fall Frolic

by Shelley Knapp, 76" x 76", 2002

Shelley had made the leaf blocks for a quilt for her husband Randy. She thought she knew exactly how she wanted to set them, until I gave her *Born Again* to quilt for me. When she asked me if I would mind if she used the set for her leaves, I encouraged her to do just that. When I saw her quilt I knew I wanted to include it in this book for all of you to see.

Primarily Primary

by Pat Marean, machine quilted by Phyllis Reddish, 58" x 58", 2002

These blocks were part of a friendship exchange, so Pat knew the blocks would not all be the same size. She chose the Two-for-One Set because of its reputation for being so forgiving. The yellow strips were chosen for all the outside blocks, with a deep red for the central block. Note again how Pat has strategically colored the triangle frames to create that star image in the center of the quilt.

It Takes a Village

by Sharyn Craig, machine quilted by Joanie Keith, 56" x 71", 1996

In this quilt, straight, dark value strips set off twelve of the blocks, while pieced triangles of very light value replaced the simple coping triangles. If you are willing to put in the time to piece the triangles, the effort really pays off. It is not difficult piecing, just time consuming. It may be the Two-for-One Set, but it sure doesn't look like it. The viewer has to work quite hard to find the set.

Autumn Splendor

by Sharyn Craig, machine quilted by Joanie Keith, 60" x 60", 1996

For this quilt I wanted to see what the effect would be if I changed the value on the strip frames. By making the value of those strips light, the same as the backgrounds of the blocks and part of the framing triangles on the alternating blocks, it makes it particularly difficult to see the piecing structure. Look at *Spumoni Sorbet* in the Gallery of Quilts (page 88) to see another interpretation of this border.

In all the quilt chapters in this book you'll see how different quilters interpreted the same setting, but in very different ways. It is easy to acknowledge that totally different blocks will obviously look different in the same setting, but aren't you impressed with how the very same blue star blocks can be made to look so totally different in spite of the same setting? Keep reading through the rest of the chapters. The fun is just beginning.

CHAPTER 3

Windblown-Square Set

"You won't find a simpler pieced frame anywhere for your blocks."

SHARYN

Windblown-Square Set

he Windblown Square pattern is a very old traditional block. I have played with this block for years, both by itself as a block pattern for an all-over quilt, and as the frame for other blocks.

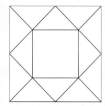

Windblown Square

Here are two of my favorite quilts using this block. In *Windy Stars*, 6" LeMoyne Star blocks were framed with the Windblown Square block pieces, while 3" appliquéd alphabet letters were set into the exact same piecing frame in *For My Baby*. The overall images look totally different due to the coloring structure, not the piecing structure.

For My Baby
by Sharyn Craig, 48" x 42", 1998

Framing Your Blocks

You won't find a simpler pieced frame anywhere for your blocks. It's so easy to create these pieces to fit any size blocks. All you need to know is the finished size of the block you're framing. To that number you add $1\frac{1}{4}$".

The $1\frac{1}{4}$" added to the original block size never changes and will work for any size block you choose to frame.

1 Measure the finished size of your focus block and add $1\frac{1}{4}$" to determine the size of the squares to use for making the framing triangles.

Windy Stars
by Sharyn Craig quilted by Joanie Keith, 47" x 47", 1998

2 Cut 3 squares that size and cut them each twice from corner to corner. The resulting triangles are the exact size you need to frame the block. *Note: To create the "windblown" look, you will need to use 2 dark or medium squares and 1 light square to make the framing triangles.*

3 Sew 4 triangles of a dark fabric to the focus block as shown.

 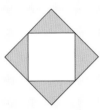

Attach the first set of triangles to the block.

TIP: *One thing to keep in mind is the grain of the fabric. The first four triangles you attach to the block will have bias grain on the outside edge, so be careful handling the blocks at this stage. I recommend waiting until the block is completely framed to iron it. You can finger-press the triangles so that the seam allowance goes toward the triangles, but ironing runs the risk of stretching and distorting the bias edges of these triangles.*

You can also convert these first triangles to the same triangle used in the Square-in-a-Square set. (Refer to page 105 for further discussion on these triangles.) Then you'll have straight of grain on the outside edge. Personally, I prefer to make all the triangles the exact same way. I've never had a problem with the bias, as long as I do not iron prematurely.

4 Lay out the remainder of the triangles to form the pattern. Sew the dark and light triangles together. I recommend sewing from the square corner of the triangle toward the point, being careful to always have the same color triangle on top as you are stitching since they are directional units. If you sew some with light on top and some with dark on top, you won't get the right pattern.

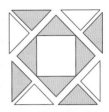

Lay out pieces to form pattern.

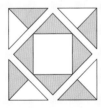

Sew triangles together from square corner to point, keeping same color triangle on top.

5 Lay out the units and sew the combined triangles to the block.

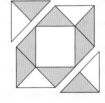 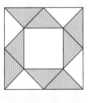

Lay out the units.   Attach the triangles.   Finished, framed block

Example: For the 6" LeMoyne Star blocks in *Windy Stars*, I cut three 7 1/4" squares for the triangles to frame each block. One of the squares was the light beige. Two of the squares were similar, but different, browns, greens, or burgundies.

I cut the squares twice diagonally into quarter-square triangles.

I sewed four of the same dark triangles to the LeMoyne Star block and continued to add the dark and light triangles to form the Windy Star frame.

Adding Coping Strips

If the blocks you're framing aren't all the same size, you can add coping strips to them first. Sometimes that additional coping piece can be an interesting color addition to the block recipe. If you don't want to draw attention to the fact that those pieces are there, remember you can use negative visibility strips, either by matching the background of the original block, or by using the same fabric as the triangles you'll add in the first round.

Setting the Blocks

The framed blocks can be set any way you like. The straight orientation of the adjacent set, also known as the side-by-side set or the tangent set, is the one you'll see most of in this chapter. The adjacent set allows opportunity for secondary designs to emerge. *For My Baby* relied on the adjacent set for the coloration to work. So did *31 Flavors* on page 30. If you had put sashing between the original framed blocks, you wouldn't have been able to see the image.

At the beginning of the chapter, I presented a single block image for you, so that we would all be on the same page as we started. Now I'm going to give you a larger, all-over Setting Map, both in the straight and diagonal orientation and complete with the border triangles on the straight set if you want to keep them.

More Ideas

Notice the triangle-frame border used on five of the quilts seen here. The exact same size triangle used to frame the blocks also created the border for *Windy Stars* on page 24, *For My Baby* on page 24, *Fairmeadow II* on page 27, *Lions and Tigers, No Bears, OH MY* on page 28, and *31 Flavors* on page 30.

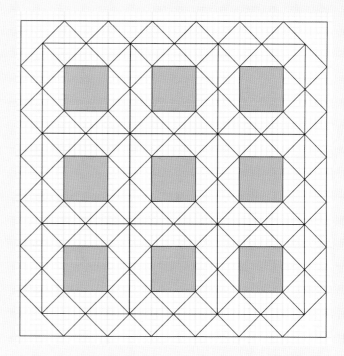

Setting Map for Windblown Square in straight-set orientation

Setting Map for Windblown Square in diagonal-set orientation

Fairmeadow II

by Sharyn Craig, 29" x 52", 1994

The appliqué images on this quilt were taken from a Jeanna Kimball pattern entitled *Fairmeadow*. I can't draw so I am delighted when people like Jeanna put out patterns that I can borrow from. I made three 6" appliqué blocks, which I set into the Windblown Square block. The stars, moon, bunny, sunflower, goat, and pear were images from Jeanna's pattern, which I scattered around the borders. I love this fun little quilt and the way I think of my friend Jeanna every time I look at it.

Follow His Star

by Sharyn Craig, 50" x 62", 2002

I designed the Santa-in-a-Star block years ago for a Christmas block exchange. It then turned into a workshop I taught for several years. These blocks were given to me by students in one of those classes. I had them for several years before finally deciding how I wanted to set them. I opted for this set so each block would get its own space. I love the way you can take twelve 6" blocks and make a nice sized wall quilt.

Make Mine Pastel

by Laurine Leeke, 71" x 59", 2002

Laurine took a set of our blue Sawtooth Stars and turned them into a very pastel quilt through the fabrics she selected for her Windblown-Square frame. She's not a blue person and really didn't want the blocks to feel blue when she finished the quilt. She likes soft, pastel colors, so for her this was a natural palette to work with. She set her framed blocks with light value sashing to further separate the blocks and give more open, light value to the finished quilt. The prairie point edge and the scrappy, inner border repeat the pastel colors.

Lions and Tigers, No Bears, OH MY

by Ruth Gordy, quilted by The Quilted Rose, 34" x 34", 2002

There may not be any bears on this quilt, but there sure are majestic lion and tiger heads. Ruth fussy-cut the animal heads from a jungle print. They weren't all the same size, or even the same shape. She ingeniously framed each of them to a 4" finished size. Inspired by the elongated pinwheel shapes in *For My Baby*, but not wanting that many pinwheels, Ruth chose to show only two green and two gold ones. This is a very striking quilt, perfect for any den or man's office wall.

Almost Antique
by Carolyn Smith, 54" x 65", 2002

Carolyn and I worked together on this variation. I actually colored the image, then handed the colored diagram to Carolyn and said, "See what you can do with this."

She worked with the blue star blocks as her focus blocks. Next, she needed to decide what colors to use in the actual quilt. The way I had colored the pink pinwheels actually gave her the push she was looking for. She'd been wanting to make a reproduction-inspired quilt from the mid 1800s in the pink and brown palette. Next thing she knew she was pulling fabric, cutting, and playing with triangles on the design wall. I didn't even recognize it as the design I had colored.

This is one of the great things about having quilts from lots of different quiltmakers that I can share with you. Each of us interprets assignments in a unique way. When we aren't limited to a specific recipe, the outcome is special each and every time.

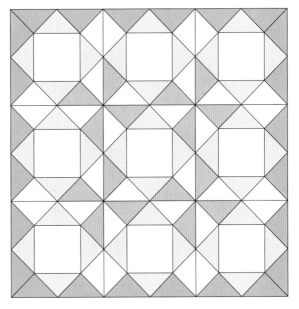

Colored diagram for Carolyn to play with

31 Flavors

by Sharyn Craig, quilted by Joann Stuebing,
33" x 33", 2002

Joann got these blocks in an Internet block swap and allowed me to play with them. I needed to do a little bit of block-size reconciliation before I could actually begin the final framing. This was one of those rare times when I chose to color on paper before I started cutting fabric because I wanted to experiment with value position and design image. I was trying to lose the Windblown Square block image and knew it would be easier to color first. I also found that the triangle border became essential to the design outcome. The actual piecing construction was exactly as the one diagrammed earlier in this chapter.

Adam's Quilt

by Sharyn Craig, machine quilted by Shelley Knapp, 64" x 81", 2002

Yes, here are more of the blue star blocks. The color recipe this time was "bright with light." I framed each of the blue stars in a different bright color and knew I wanted to put them on point. Rather than using plain, side setting triangles, I pieced the modified nine-patch chain image. This reduced the amount of light fabric in the setting triangles and also made the quilt much more interesting. I was thinking of my grandson, Adam, when pulling the fabrics for this quilt. It will go on the twin bed in my guestroom for him to sleep under when staying with Gramma.

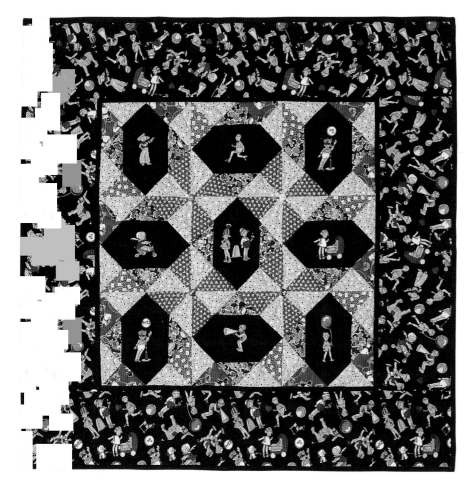

Little People

by Connie Chunn, 22 $1/2$" x 22 $1/2$", 2002

Connie began with the fabric you see in the border. She fussy-cut each child from the fabric and then built a black background around the child using a crazy-quilt, log cabin, foundation-piecing technique. Then she used both antique and reproduction 30s fabrics to create the Windblown Square. She strategically used black fabric as two of the original triangles on the square, rotating them on every other block. She embellished the blocks with four buttons sewn in the centers of the red and blue middle pinwheels. The black elongated hexagon images are so dramatic that the viewer has trouble seeing the Windblown-Square image in this fun and playful quilt.

What other setting options can you come up with for the framed blocks? There are some chapters in this book that incorporate an alternating block with the focus block. How about putting the framed block from this chapter alternately with a Chain block or a Crossover block? Or maybe you could set these framed blocks into a Garden-Maze Set? The possibilities are only as limited as your imagination. I'm providing you with the basic tools you need. Now it's up to you to see what you can do with them.

Square-in-a-Square Set

*"Instead of
using a straight
set, you might
opt to put your
blocks on point."*

SHARYN

Square-in-a-Square Set

 his set is a simple alternating block set up. Your focus blocks will alternate with the simple Square-in-a-Square connector block.

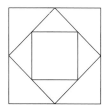

Square-in-a-Square

It's so easy to make the connector block any size you need it to be. The size of this block depends on the finished size of your focus blocks. The finished size of the pieces you need for the Square-in-a-Square block are exactly half the measurement of the finished size of your original, or focus, block. Using this easy formula, if you had 6" focus blocks you would need a 3" square, a 3" quarter-square triangle, and a 3" half-square triangle.

6" finished focus block.

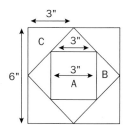

6" finished Square-in-a-Square, 3" square (A), 3" quarter-square inner triangle (B), 3" half-square outer triangle (C).

Making the Block

1 Measure the finished size of your focus block and divide that number by 2 to determine the finished sizes of the square and triangles in the Square-in-the-Square connector block.

What if your focus blocks aren't all the same size? Add coping strips, of course!

2 To determine the cut sizes of the pieces in the Square-in-the-Square block:

- Add $1/2$" to the finished square size and cut a square.

Finished square size + $^1/_2$"

- Add $1^1/_4$" to the length of the long side of the finished quarter-square inner triangle. Cut 1 square to that size and cut it twice from corner to corner to yield 4 triangles.

Finished triangle size + $1^1/_4$"

- Add $^7/_8$" to the short side of the finished half-square outer triangle and cut 2 squares to that size. Cut the squares from corner to corner to yield a total of 4 triangles.

Finished triangle size + $^7/_8$"

3 Sew 2 quarter-square triangles to opposite sides of the square. Add the remaining quarter-square triangles to the other sides of the square. See the tip on page 25 for information on pressing the block at this point.

4 Sew the 2 half-square triangles to opposite sides of the unit. Add the remaining half-square triangles to the other sides of the unit. Iron the block well.

Example: To make the Square-in-a-Square block for a 6" focus block, you will need to cut one 3 $\frac{1}{2}$" square, two 3 $\frac{7}{8}$" squares, and one 4 $\frac{1}{4}$" square. Cut the 3 $\frac{7}{8}$" squares once diagonally and the 4 $\frac{1}{4}$" square twice diagonally.

Setting the Blocks

The basic overall Setting Map for this quilt might look like this:

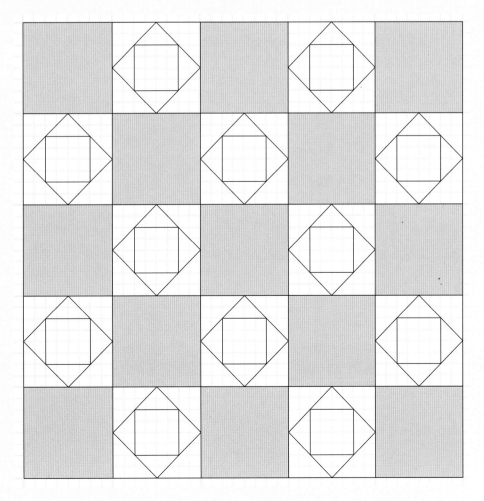

Square-in-a-Square set straight, starting and ending with focus blocks

Remember, when you set the blocks in the straight orientation, you normally need to have an odd number of blocks in each direction to give balance to the quilt design.

Instead of using a straight set, you might opt to put your blocks on point. In that case you can have any number of blocks in either direction.

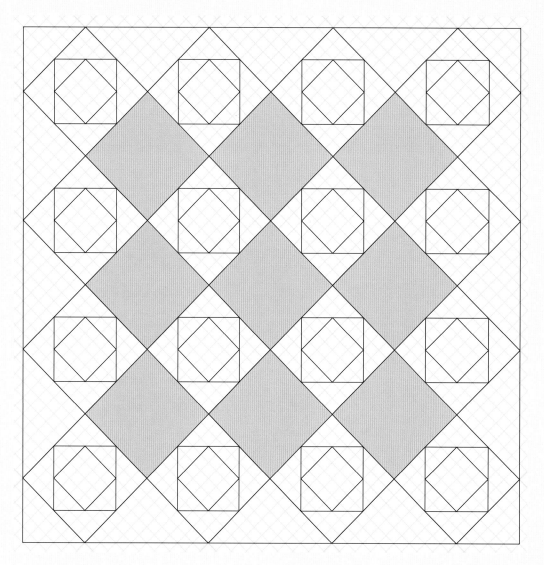

Square-in-a-Square set diagonally, starting and ending with Square-in-a-Square blocks

More Ideas

Looking at the quilts using this set you will see both some traditional interpretations of the basic set as well as some variations that are not so traditional. How many other variations do you think you can come up with?

Shades of Red, White, and Blue

by Sandy Andersen, quilted by The Quilted
Rose, 48" x 48", 2002

Sandy used careful coloration of
the half-square triangles to create the
secondary star image surrounding
each of the original Sawtooth Star
blocks. Her assignment was to make
her basic blue blocks into a patriotic
quilt. Using the colors she selected,
the flag fabric in the alternating
block, plus the border, she definitely
succeeded in creating a quilt with a
flair for stirring up a march in each
of us.

Tropical Punch

by Sharyn Craig, 42" x 42", 2002

I had some LeMoyne Star blocks with
a tropical feeling that I was searching
for a fun way to set, and the Square-
in-a-Square alternate block seemed
perfect. I used a triangle frame border
around the edge of the basic quilt.
The border quarter-square triangles
are exactly the same size as the ones
in the Square-in-a-Square block. What
could be simpler? Appliquéing the
word "Aloha" to the bottom left corner
helped push that tropical feel I was
going for.

Baby Dresdens

by Sharyn Craig, quilted by Shelley Knapp,
50" x 50", 2002

I used a modified version of the map to create *Baby Dresdens*. I appliquéd the 6" Dresden Plate blocks over a period of several months as I traveled from place to place teaching. I found them to be the perfect take-along project for evenings on the road. I made seventeen blocks, and thirteen blocks fit perfectly in the body of the quilt, leaving me four blocks to use for the border corners.

The easiest way to create the modified block is to cut a square the size of the focus block with seam allowances. Then, using the Corner Cutter technique described in Chapter 10, eliminate one corner from each square. My replacement triangle was the same as the half-square triangle from the Square-in-a-Square block, or exactly half the size of the block. A 6" finished square needs a 3" Corner Cutter and a 3" replacement half-square triangle.

Modified block

Notice how I used the same triangle border as in *Tropical Punch* on page 37. I created a secondary star illusion in the center of the quilt by selecting peach fabrics for those triangles. This quilt was carefully arranged on the flannel wall before I started taking the units down to sew.

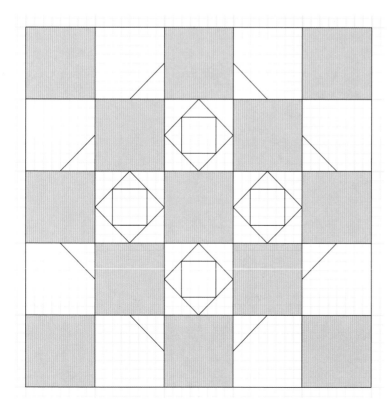

Setting Map for the modified Square-in-a-Square setting

Garden of Blooms

by Mary Pavlovich, quilted by Cindy Myers,
42" x 42", 2002

Using the technique called "Mirror-Image Magic" from a book by Bethany S. Reynolds, Mary made these fun, floral blocks. But, as many of us already know, making the blocks is the easy part. Finding a setting that pulls those blocks together can be quite another matter. Mary decided to play with the structure of *Baby Dresdens* on page 38. No longer is this just another quilt, but instead, with the playful setting and bright teals and purple, she has a great quilt.

Starlight Rhapsody

by Marnie Santos, 62" x 62", 2002

Marnie had the assignment to create a quilt in a monochromatic color scheme using her blue star blocks. She further modified even the inside Square-in-a-Square blocks by eliminating the inner pieces. Using either two or four Corner Cutters on the original cut square gave her the modified blocks she needed to create this illusion. Don't you love the way she carried that icy blue fabric out into the borders, giving that secondary square image to the quilt?

These quilts all happen to be square. How would you elongate the design for a rectangular format? The blocks are also all set in a straight-set orientation. Perhaps you might want to experiment with setting your blocks on point. What other modifications to the original Square-in-a-Square block can you come up with that might better suit your quilt design? Remember, there are no rules, just guidelines. Be inspired by the photographs, but create your own quilt.

CHAPTER 5

Chain Set

*"The possible
variations are
wonderful, both
for the simple
Chain block
as well as
how you deal
with the focus
block."*

SHARYN

Chain Set

ere we have another alternating block set to play with. In the last chapter we worked with the Square-in-a-Square alternate block. In this setting, we will use the Chain block as the alternate block to go with your focus blocks. I hope you'll enjoy this setting as much as I did while working on the quilts. The possible variations are wonderful, both for the simple Chain block as well as how you deal with the focus block.

Chain Block Variations

Some possibilities for the Chain block include:

Simple nine-patch

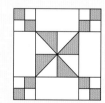

Four-patch corners, four-patch center

Four-patch corners, solid square center

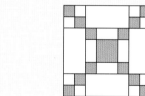

Four-patch corners, modified nine-patch center

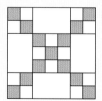

Four-patch corners, nine-patch center

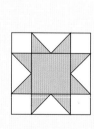

Four-patch corners, pinwheel center

These are just a few of the ways you might break down the space and be able to create the effect of the chain pieces surrounding your focus blocks. This is a set that creates a delightful frame around the blocks, while still leaving them plenty of visual room.

Some of the chains, such as the simple nine-patch, are based on equal divisions across the block, while others are based on unequal divisions. You can make the divisions however you need them to be so they will fit with, and be the same size as, your focus blocks.

Once again, with the alternating block setup, if you want to set the blocks straight, then you need to plan an odd number of blocks in each direction to create a sense of completion and balance. Blocks set straight have the chain running diagonally through the quilt. If you opt to put your blocks on point, then you can have any number of blocks in either direction. On-point blocks have the chain running parallel to the sides of the quilt. Quilts can start with either the Chain blocks or the focus blocks. You will see examples of both variations in this chapter.

Looking at the Focus Blocks

If you study the focus blocks in the quilts in this chapter, you will see that you have two different treatments to choose from. Some of the focus blocks stand on their own and are the same size as the Chain block (A), while others are framed with triangles first (B).

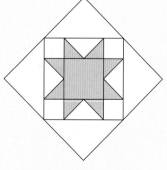

(A) stand alone   (B) framed with triangles

Chain Set Variations

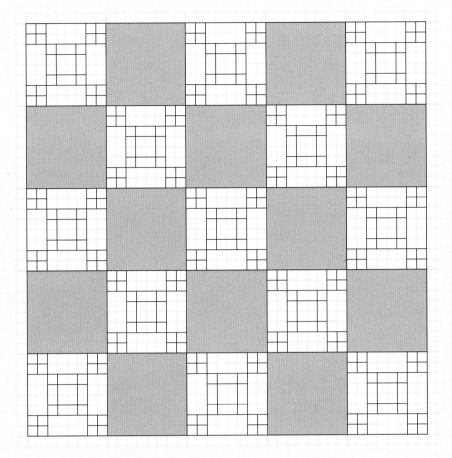

Basic Chain Set with blocks set straight in the A version

Basic Chain Set with blocks set diagonally in the A version

ADVICE FROM SHARYN:
My definition of a successful quilt is one in which you see the whole quilt first, then your eye can move around the quilt and see all the little nuances. If there is not a feeling of continuity and "wholeness" to the quilt, then I don't view it as successful.

Basic Chain Set with blocks set straight in the B version

The blocks don't have to sit next to each other, as the previous diagrams would suggest. You can add sashing to the equation. The sashing can be simple straight strips or it can be pieced. Sashing not only increases the size of the overall quilt, but it can also add interest to the design.

Color

Color can play a major part in this setting. For instance, if all the background fabric behind the focus blocks and in the Chain blocks is the same, then construction lines tend to disappear and you make a quilt that looks technically very difficult, when in reality it is amazingly simple. If your backgrounds change, then the viewer is able to see the construction path. Studying the quilts in this chapter is one way for you to get a feeling for some of the options.

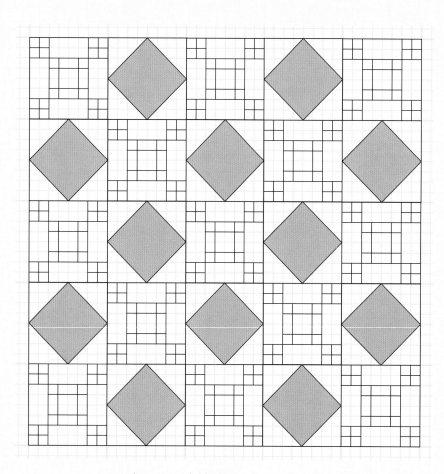

Basic Chain Set with blocks set diagonally, version B

Making and Sewing the Block

A chain needs three sections, but the sections don't have to be equal size. There will be four corners, which are all equal in size, and a center, which can be the same size as the corners or it can be different. There are four side pieces that are the same length as the center section and the same width as the corner sections.

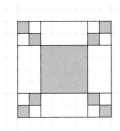

Center is larger than the corners.

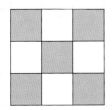

Center is the same size as the corners.

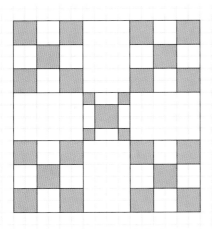

Center is smaller than the corners.

Designing the Chain Block

One of the simplest ways I've found to approach working with the chain is to draw a square the size of your focus block on graph paper and design the chain block using the small squares on the graph paper as your guide.

1 Decide that each small square on the graph paper is equal to 1" in your block and draw a large square equal to the size of your focus block. (For example, if you have an 8" focus block, you would draw your large square 8 small squares by 8 small squares on the graph paper. If you have a 6" block, you'd draw 6 squares by 6 squares.)

> **TIP:** *When designing more complex Chain blocks, you may choose to make each square on the graph paper equal to $^1/_2$" or $^1/_4$" of your block.*

2 Shade the segments of the Chain block in a design you like. Either use one of my suggestions on page 42 or create one of your own.

3 Once you have a design you like, it is easy to determine the size of the pieces needed to make the Chain block. Look at your drawn block to see how many graph paper squares you have used for each piece, convert the number of squares into inches and add $^1/_2$" for seam allowances. For example, if your center square is 2 squares x 2 squares, your piece is a 2" square and you will need to cut a piece $2^1/_2$" x $2^1/_2$".

If you use a pinwheel as your center section, add $^7/_8$" to the measurement to determine the size squares you will cut into half-square triangles.

> **TIP:** *Some Chain-block designs work better with certain block sizes because the numbers are easier to calculate. Just experiment until you have one that will work for you.*

If you haven't made the focus blocks yet, you could start with the Chain block and work backwards, determining what blocks you want to make and what size they need to be. Remember you can always add coping strips or triangles to make the size of the focus block easy to work with. See page 9 for detailed information on adding coping strips or triangles.

Doing the Math

Let's look at some examples for dealing with both the focus blocks and the alternating Chain blocks of different sizes. Let's use the 6" blue Sawtooth Star blocks and work through some options.

When you put the 6" star block on point and add triangles, the new block is 8 1/2". See Chapter 10, "Corner Triangles for Square-in-a-Square Triangles" for information on how to determine the triangle sizes. In this case, the triangles needed to frame the star would be 4 1/4" half-square triangles. You cut two 5 1/8" squares, and then cut each square corner to corner to create these triangles.

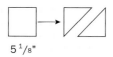

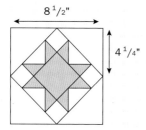

6" star focus block with framing triangles

To create an 8 1/2" Chain block for this focus block, you will need to draw a full-sized 8 1/2" square on your graph paper and divide it into the appropriate sections. In this example we made a 3" nine-patch center (1" for each nine-patch square), and 2 3/4" four patches in the corners (1 3/8" for each four-patch square). The side rectangles are 3" x 2 3/4".

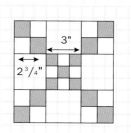

8 1/2" chain block with 3" nine-patch in the center and 2 3/4" four patches in the corners

 TIP: *Remember, we are always talking in finished numbers when doing these calculations. You must add seam allowances to each of these numbers.*

What if you'd rather work with a 9" Chain block to make the pieces fit equal divisions? By far the easiest way to accomplish this is to add oversized coping triangles to the 6" block, then square it up to 9 1/2".

Another Option

Perhaps you want framing triangles and accent coping strips like Sandy used when she made *Stars at Nite* on page 51. It may feel like we're working backwards on this example, but stay with me, I promise it works.

For this example let's begin with the Chain block. Let's make a 10 1/2" finished Chain block.

The framing triangles needed for the original blocks would be 5 1/4" half-square triangles, half the size of the Chain block. (Cutting size is 6 1/8" squares, cut once corner to corner to create the triangles, 5 1/4" + 7/8" = 6 1/8".)

Next we need to determine what size square fits inside those 5 1/4" triangles. To find the long side of the 5 1/4" triangle, multiply: 5.25" x 1.414 = 7.4235". (The long side of any half-square triangle is always 1.414 times the length of the short side, no matter what size the triangle is.)

That is the finished size of the inner square, but Sandy had 6" Sawtooth Star blocks. To make her star blocks big enough to fit inside these triangles we need coping strips. To determine how wide the coping strip needs to be, subtract your block size from the inner square size you determined above.

7.4235" − 6" = 1.4235"

Divide that number in half (for each side) then add the $1/2$" seam allowance.

1.4235" ÷ 2 = .7117" (finished width of coping strip)
.7117" + .5" = 1.2117" (cut width of coping strip)

As a quilter I would use this information to cut the coping strips 1 $1/4$". I would frame the star and iron well. To square up the block to the size needed, you will go back to your original calculations and determine the block size.

.7117" (finished width of 1 coping strip) + .7117" (finished width of 2nd coping strip) + 6" block + .5" (seam allowance) = 7.9235".

This is the raw-edge-to-raw-edge size that the framed star would need to be to work with the 5 $1/4$" corner triangles.

How would a quilter use this number? We can't easily cut 7 $9/10$" with our rotary rulers, but we can cut the framed stars a "short" 8". This is bigger than 7 $7/8$", but not all the way to 8". This would give us almost a 1" strip frame showing.

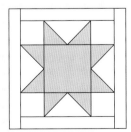

Framed block, squared up to a short 8"

Sew the 5 $1/4$" half-square triangles (cut from the 6 $1/8$" squares) to each side of the framed star, and then trim the final block to 11", or a finished 10 $1/2$", to match our Chain block.

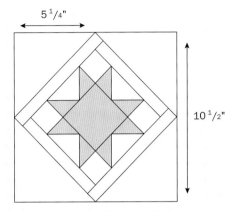

Star block with coping strips and corner triangles

The Chain block is a finished 10 $1/2$". This divides into 3 equal parts of 3 $1/2$" each. You would have 3 $1/2$" finished four patches, and a 3 $1/2$" center unit. In Sandy's quilt, she made that center unit a pinwheel. The finished size of the triangles needed for the pinwheel is 1 $3/4$".

More Ideas

Now let's look at some quilts made in the Chain Set and see how versatile this setting can be.

Pinwheel Chain

by Sharyn Craig, quilted by Gem Taylor,
60" x 74 $\frac{1}{2}$", 1998

This quilt was inspired by one made
in the 1930s. I saw a picture of a quilt
and set about figuring out ways to
create a similar illusion easily and
efficiently. The Pinwheel blocks are
framed with triangles, then set to
alternate with the Chain block. The
Chain block is based on equal
divisions of a 9" space. There are 3"
four patches, a 3" nine patch and
some 3" solid squares. I made the
chain very scrappy because the
pinwheels were all similar greens
and white. The blocks are set straight
starting with the chain block.

Peony Chain

by Sharyn Craig, 56" x 56", 1998

I love the way the Peony blocks
appear to be drifting across the
surface. I could have oriented them
all in the same direction, but decided
it would be more interesting to make
them turn differently. Since the flower
blocks were all scrappy, I made the
chain in the controlled soft green
palette. Once again the blocks are
set straight beginning with the Chain
block. I also continued the chain a
little further into the initial border
with another set of four patches
and some of the background fabric
connecting them.

Right Out of Mother's Parlor

by Marnie Santos, 60" x 79", 2002

Here you have more of the blue Sawtooth Star blocks. This time they are set with fabrics that make the quilt look straight out of the 19th century. Where the previous two quilts concentrated on a dark chain with light backgrounds, Marnie chose to make her chain light and the backgrounds lots and lots of different dark value reproduction-style fabrics. She thought the finished quilt had a Victorian feel to it, which explains her name for the quilt.

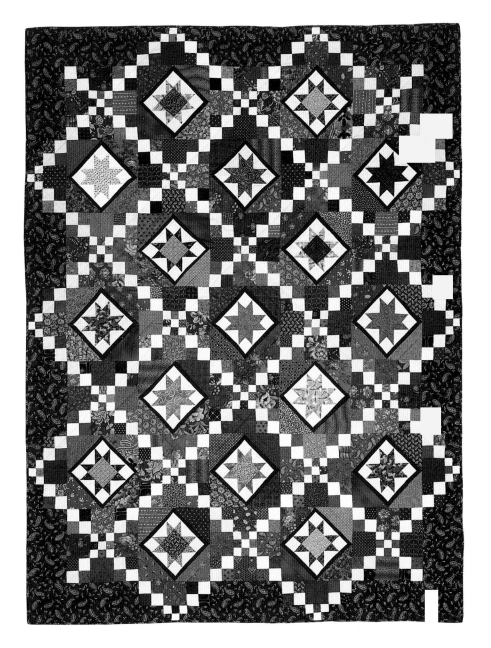

Sampler Chain

by Sharyn Craig, quilted by Wendy Knight,
63" x 82", 2002

The blocks are on point and start with the focus blocks. Note how the chain is parallel to the edges of the quilt when the blocks are on the diagonal. This gives a very different effect to the finished quilt. The focus blocks have a different background than the framing triangles and the background in the Chain blocks. When the triangle-framed blocks are set on point, the original focus blocks are oriented in the straight position. Piecing the setting triangles also creates the illusion of a much more difficult pieced structure than there actually is.

ADVICE FROM SHARYN: *All the blocks in this sampler-style quilt can be found in Chapter 10, which includes block patterns, just in case you don't have blocks that are already made, just lying around waiting to be used!*

Stars at Nite

by Sandy Andersen, machine quilted by Wendy Knight, 53" x 74", 2002

It's hard to believe you're seeing those same little blue star blocks again. Sandy's color assignment was to create a finished quilt that was "bright, primary, and black." I love the way she colored the chain pieces to create different rows of color. Notice that this quilt has no additional border. When the top was done to this point, Sandy auditioned several different possibilities. She finally decided to listen to the quilt, which was loudly trying to tell her that it was done just the way it was. Learn to listen to your quilts.

Royal Crossing

by Sharyn Craig, 72" x 74", 2001

The Royal Cross block is a beautiful old traditional block featuring gentle curved seaming. My goal for this quilt was to minimize the curved illusion. By sashing the blocks and alternating them with the Chain blocks, I achieved the effect I was looking for. I used Pinwheel blocks, not only at the center of the Chain blocks, but also at the cornerstone intersections. I found that these two blocks worked quite well together because both of them created the corner-to-corner visual connection. The quilt gives an unexpected final result to some fun blocks.

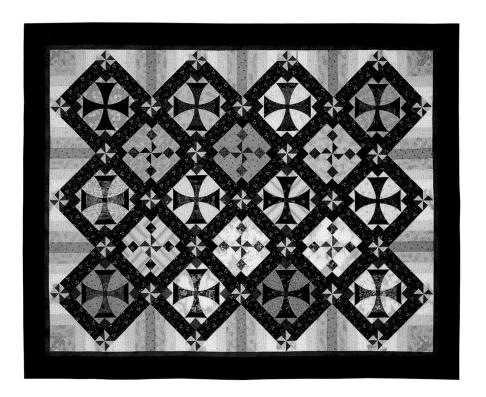

Prairie Baskets

by Irene Mueller, 70" x 92", 2002

The Prairie Star Basket blocks are from Judy Martin's book, *The Block Book*.

In the spring of 2002, I had a teaching trip to the St. Louis, Missouri area. I stayed with Irene, who took me in her sewing room where the basket blocks were on the flannel design wall. She commented how the blocks had been there for awhile, waiting for inspiration. I could see these Basket blocks would be perfect for the Chain Set, so I introduced her to the basic chain concept and invited her to make a quilt for this book. She played up the illusion of the star where the pieced sashing intersects at the corners.

"Every time I teach a class, I start new blocks for the demonstration. I've got lots of those, but now, thanks to your inventive way of working, I know I'll be able to finish them. See what an influence you are! I just love the way you challenge people with all your ideas. "

Irene Mueller, Kirkwood, Missouri

Paisley Festival

by Mary Pavlovich, quilted by Marge Goumas,
56" x 56", 2002

Mary had the five sampler blocks
stashed away in a closet. She'd made
them as class samples and didn't want
to make any more. But what do you do
with five blocks? She decided to make
a light chain on dark background. I
think it's great the way she took some
very blue blocks and made a black,
red, and gray quilt from those blocks.
She didn't add any more blue but kept
the gray tone to help the blocks merge
into the new colors.

Now it's your turn to play. Get out the
blocks you want to work with, then
start pulling fabric for the Chain
blocks. Next think about how you
want to color the Chain blocks to
create your special effect. Once you've
done that, the rest will just start falling
into place. For this quilt, doodling on
graph paper, shading in the squares,
is a good way both to help you
better visualize what's going to happen,
and to resolve the math involved.
Remember, quilting is fun, so let's
start playing.

CHAPTER 6

Crossover Set

"I hope
you're going to
enjoy the
flexibility and
design options
possible with
this block and
ultimately
the set."

SHARYN

es, it's another alternating set. This time our alternate block is a simple "X" shape.

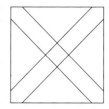

"X" block

"X" Block Variations

I hope you're going to enjoy the flexibility and design options possible with this block and ultimately the set. One thing that is really fun about this block is that you can make the X skinny or fat. Or how about skinny one direction and fat the other? You can color the block in two fabrics, or lots of fabrics. You can make the X light and the triangles dark. Or, if you prefer, you can color the triangles light and the X dark. You can set the blocks straight or on point. You're in charge.

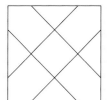

Block with a fat X

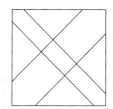

Block that has a fat diagonal in one direction and a skinny diagonal in the other

Block with a light X

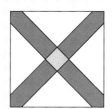

Block with a dark X

Setting Options

Since this is an alternate set, the same guidelines hold true here as in the previous two chapters. If you set the blocks straight, use an odd number of blocks in each direction for the quilt to have balance and appear "finished." If you set your blocks on point, you can have any number of blocks in either direction.

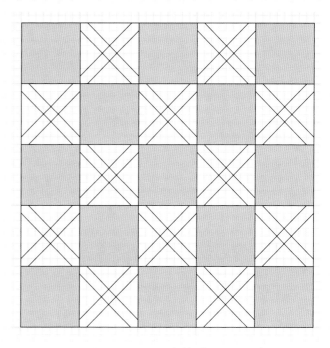

Basic Crossover Set with blocks set straight

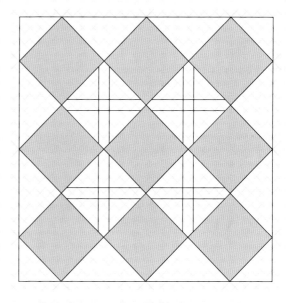

Basic Crossover Set with blocks set on point

Designing the Block

When I begin the design phase using this setting, I find it helpful to draw the X block full size. Start with a large enough sheet of graph paper to accommodate a square the size of your focus block. You may need to tape multiple sheets of graph paper together.

1 Draw a square on the graph paper the finished size of the focus block.

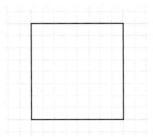

Draw a square the size of the finished focus block.

2 From each corner measure in both directions, anywhere from $1/4$" to 2" and make marks on the edge of the square. This distance depends on the effect you're looking for and the size of your focus blocks. The farther from the corner you measure, the fatter your X will be. Mark the other corners in the same way.

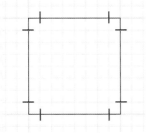

Make marks on the edge.

3 Connect those marks diagonally across the block.

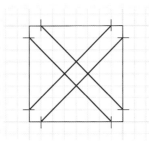

Connect the marks.

Drawing the block full size is the best way to actually see the scale you're dealing with. I sometimes pin that graph paper square to the flannel wall between the blocks to see how the size of the X feels with the focus block. If I like what I see, I stay with what I've drawn. If it doesn't feel right, I repeat the exercise, either increasing or decreasing the distance from the corner to the marks.

Cutting the Pieces and Making the Block

The standard X block requires three pieces: the edge triangles (A), the square-on-point (B), and the pointy pieces (C).

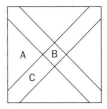

You will probably need to use templates to make some of the pieces for the X block. (See page 111 for information about the template material I heartily recommend, which is 100% rotary friendly). Since some of the shapes used aren't easily cut using the math formulas for rotary cutting, I find making a template the fastest and most accurate method for both cutting and piecing the block to the size I need.

Drafting and making templates is not difficult once you get used to the process. Being able to make your own rotary-friendly templates can be an invaluable technique.

the exact length of the long side of the triangle on your graph-paper drawing. Add 1 $\frac{1}{4}$" to that number. Cut a square that size, and cut it twice from corner to corner. Each square yields the 4 triangles you need to complete the X block.

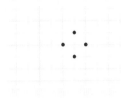

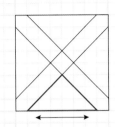

Measurement of long side of triangle

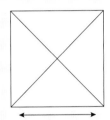

Measurement of long side of triangle + 1 $\frac{1}{4}$" = size to cut square

2 The square-on-point (B) can be cut with a template, or see page 111 for more information on a specialty ruler that can be used to cut this square.

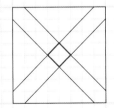

b. Connect the dots.

c. Add a $\frac{1}{4}$" seam allowance and turn it into a usable template.

d. Place the edge of the template on the straight of grain of the fabric and cut 1 center square piece (B) for each block.

3 The pointy piece (C) is definitely best cut with a template. After you've drawn it on graph paper, it's easy to determine the measurements needed to create the template. I prefer to take a new piece of graph paper and use a dot-to-dot technique, rather than trying to trace the original.

a. Start at the top point and make a dot (1) on the graph paper to represent that point. Next, using the increment you selected on the original drawing, measure over in both directions from that point and make 2 more dots (2) and (3).

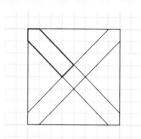

Note the locations of the point and corners on the graph paper.

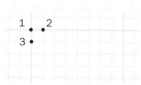

Use a second sheet of graph paper to mark dots at upper point and corners.

b. Look back at your original drawing and determine how to get from that new dot to the bottom corner. Study the graph paper...it is usually "over so many inches, and down so many inches." Now take that information to the new graph paper and measure the "over and down" from dot 2 and put a dot (4). Measure the same amount from dot 3 and mark a dot (5).

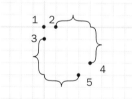

Measure over and down from dots 2 and 3 to place dots 4 and 5.

c. Next, connect all the dots.

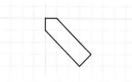

Connect the dots.

d. Add a 1/4" seam allowance to all the edges of the shape you have drawn. Your pattern piece is complete. Turn it into a usable template with material of your choice, and you'll be ready to cut fabric.

Add 1/4" seam allowance to all sides.

e. Place the long edge of the template on the straight of grain of the fabric and cut 4 pointy pieces (C) for each block.

4 Sew the square (B) between 2 pointy pieces (C). Press.

5 Sew a pointy piece (C) between 2 triangles (A). Press. Repeat with the remaining pointy piece (C) and triangles.

6 Sew a A/C/A unit to each side of the C/B/C unit. Iron the block well.

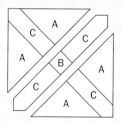

ADVICE FROM SHARYN: *Before you cut enough pieces to make the blocks for the entire quilt, I recommend cutting only enough pieces for one block and sewing them together to make sure they fit properly and look just right. Nothing is more frustrating than spending hours cutting everything out, only to discover you created the template improperly or did the math incorrectly.*

More Ideas

Now let's look at some more quilts that also use the Crossover Set.

Sandy had these blue Quiltmaker's Star blocks from a friendship block exchange several years earlier. I offered to play with her blocks and set them together. The biggest design change was to add some triangles of the light green background fabric and dark blue fabric, using them on the four corners for interest. I love the way this setting gives the illusion that the blocks are on point with diagonal sashing. It is so hard for the viewer to find the actual construction lines in this setting.

Crossed Colors
by Sharyn Craig, quilted by Joanie Keith,
61" x 61", 1999

I received the color blocks in this quilt from a color design block exchange. Since many different quilters made the blocks, I had a size issue to clean up first. I used blue coping strips around each block. I wanted them to show and become a part of the design. I didn't want the X blocks to penetrate the border, but I did want the colors to finish as square images. It was critical that I take the X blocks down from the flannel design wall one at a time and be very careful not to mix up the order of the colors.

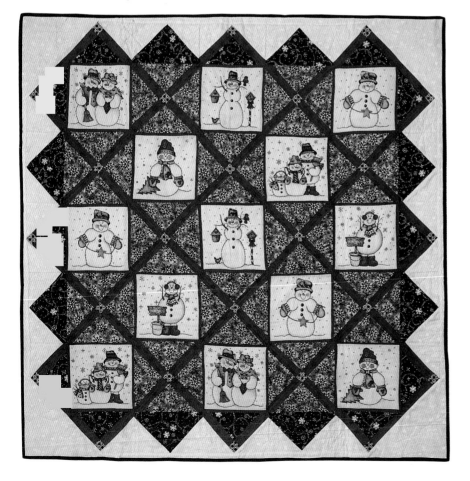

Celebrating Snow
by Marnie Santos, 41" x 41", 2002

Marnie purchased the snowmen panel years ago and had it tucked away in the back of her closet. Then one day at quilt guild she won a packet of fabric with snowflake and snowmen images all over it. Add the snowmen panel and my Setting Maps, and she was half way to a quilt! The narrow red frame around each of the snowmen made the red fabric the perfect choice for the X's in the Crossover block. She played both on graph paper and on the flannel wall until she was satisfied that the quilt felt finished.

You may remember *31 Flavors* on page 30. This is another quilt made with more of those 4" blocks. Joann enlarged the original blocks with log cabin stripping, red strips on two sides, and beige on the other two. Next, she added a framing strip of black for graphic emphasis. She used that same black for the X pieces, which creates the illusion of looking through a window. Remember, she had the blocks for years waiting for the right inspiration to strike.

◆ ADVICE FROM SHARYN: *I know it's easy to get burdened with guilt because you have lots of blocks sitting around. You feel like you shouldn't start new projects because of these unfinished ones. Just keep telling yourself that good things are worth waiting for, but maybe now is a good time to check your closets to see what blocks are lurking there. Maybe you've found the inspiration you've been waiting for!*

Romantic Garden

by Sharyn Craig, quilted by Shirley Greenhoe
64" x 74", 2002

Pat Marean's quilt *Primarily Primary* on page 21 and this quilt were both made from the same blocks. The block is actually called The Romantic Age, and was designed by Judy Martin and seen in her book *The Block Book*. A group of my quilt friends exchanged these really bright blocks in 2001. I wanted to calm the blocks down, so I chose a field of medium to dark greens, which can be a very calming color. The quilt ended up with a very garden-like feeling, hence the name I chose for it.

They're back...Those blue Sawtooth Star blocks return again. Ruth's assignment, in addition to the Crossover Set, was to create an Oriental feeling for her quilt. She found fabric with Koi fish and used it to pull her other colors.

Notice how Ruth's quilt "breaks the rule." Here we have an alternating set with the blocks set straight, featuring an odd number of blocks one direction and an even number the other direction. This is a very strong quilt with lots of things going on to attract the viewer's eye back again and again.

"It's so exciting to watch these quilts come alive. I would never have believed we could each take the same set of simple blue star blocks and make them into such totally different quilts."
Sandy Andersen, El Cajon, California

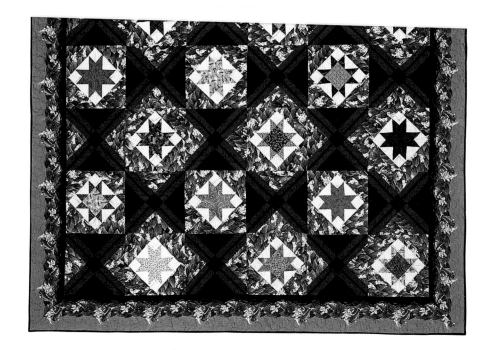

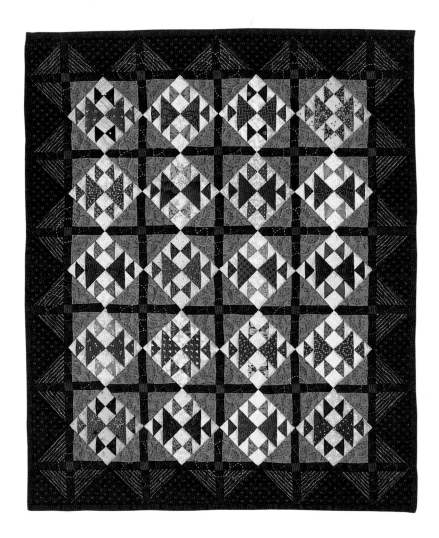

Jan's Favorite
by Connie Chunn, 16" x 19", 2002

Connie started with twenty 2 1/2" Fox and Geese blocks. She put them on point, alternating with the Crossover block. Careful and deliberate coloration for the outside Crossover blocks gave the quilt a built-in border all its own. Even though the final setting triangles are a different fabric, the viewer has to look really carefully to actually see that. This is a striking, but warm and friendly quilt.

Now it's your turn. Have you been thinking of some blocks you might want to try this setting out on? I sure hope so. I know you could play with this setting over and over again and not make the same quilt twice. The options are only as limited as your imagination, so have fun and start playing!

Garden-Maze Set

"This is a
great setting
to use whether
you have all
the same
blocks or a
collection of
different blocks."
SHARYN

We'll refer to this set as the Garden Maze because you can create quilts that look exactly like that familiar old-time sashing; however, you can also create quilts that look absolutely nothing like the Garden Maze. That's what's totally awesome about the way we will do the piecing structure.

Another benefit of this construction technique is that it allows you to reconcile block sizes where necessary. The initial framing strips are coping strips that become part of the set itself. This construction technique is significantly easier to piece than the original method, which required either appliqué or templates similar to the ones in the Crossover block in Chapter 6 to connect the blocks.

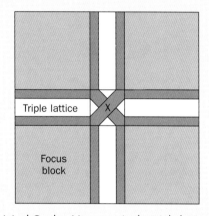

Original Garden Maze required a triple lattice and the X block for the cornerstone.

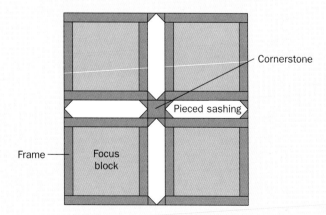

Modified Garden-Maze piecing

This is a great setting to use whether you have all the same blocks or a collection of different blocks. It is a setting that allows your eyes to see each block independently as well as take in the quilt as a whole. Another benefit of this setting is that it can make your quilt significantly larger than the size your original blocks might indicate.

Framing strips can be one color or lots of different colors. They can be light value or dark value. When you want to see stars at the intersections, you'll color your cornerstones the same as the triangles. Those stars can be subtle, like you see in the quilt called *Compromise* on page 72, or they can be strong and dramatic, like you see in *Patriotic Games* on page 74 and *Pathway to the Stars* on page 74.

I never get tired of playing with a set and trying to make it look totally different each time I use it. *Pastel Pinwheels* is yet another example of this set and the different illusion created through coloration.

Pastel Pinwheel
by Sharyn Craig, quilted by Joanie Keith, 54" x 54", 2001

from a Four-Patch block that had opposing blue and green squares. This coloration created the illusion of cross-connecting the blocks through color. Some people look at this quilt and can imagine a linked-circle effect.

"Since I've gotten to know Sharyn, I look at quilts very differently. She has opened my eyes to setting blocks in a totally different way. Working on her quilts, especially those I had the opportunity to see as just blocks first, has totally inspired me."

Shelley Knapp, Brookings, Oregon

Getting Started

Before we look at and study more quilts, I'll give you some starting guidelines for the size to cut strips and the construction technique, but these are only a beginning. Feel free to make changes as your blocks seem to need.

We'll start working with our blocks by framing them with a strip. Next we'll create sashing pieces with triangles at the corners. The cornerstone is a solid square.

and 1 ½" (*Field of Greens*). Most of the quilts have a finished 1 ¼" frame.

1 For the cut framing pieces, you know you must add ½" to the finished piece size, but I recommend an additional ¼"–½" when you need to reconcile size. For a 1" finished frame, you would want to cut 1 ¾"–2" strips. For a 1 ½" finished frame, you would cut 2 ¼"–2 ½" strips.

> **TIP:** *If your blocks are significantly different in size, you may need to add coping strips to the smaller ones prior to working with the framing strips for the actual set.*

2 Sew the strips onto the block, adding strips to opposite sides of the block and trimming the length even with the block. Add the 2 remaining strips in the same way. Iron the block well.

3 Using a square-up ruler, trim the block to the desired size. Remember the desired size is finished size plus ½" for seam allowances.

Sashing Strips

The guideline here is that the finished sashing is twice the width of the finished frame, so if you had a 1" finished frame, the finished sashing would be 2" wide. If you had a 1 ½" finished frame, you would need 3" finished sashing strips. Remember, this is a guideline. You certainly can have more space between the blocks if you desire. In fact, more space is often nice on larger blocks.

1 Cut the sashing strips the finished sashing width plus ½" for seam allowances by the length of the framed block (raw edge to raw edge).

2 Cut the number of sashing strips you need for your quilt.

TIP: *You will not need four sashing strips for each block because one sashing strip is used between two blocks. You may want to lay out the blocks on a design wall in your set and then count the number of sashing strips you will need or refer to the chart on page 108.*

Sashing Triangles

The finished size of the sashing triangles is one-half the width of the finished sashing. If you had a 2" finished sashing, you would need 1" finished triangles. If you had a 2 1/2" finished sashing, you would need 1 1/4" finished triangles. See below for the two options for making these triangles.

Sashing Construction

You could construct the triangles on the corners of the sashing pieces by sewing squares diagonally across each corner of the sashing strip, or you could use the Corner Cutter technique (page 106) to eliminate the corners from the sashing strip and then attach replacement triangles. Choose the one that works best for you.

If you are constructing triangles by sewing a square corner to corner to the ends of the sashing strip, cut squares the finished triangle size plus 1/2". You will need 4 squares for each sashing strip that will be connected to another block. (You do not have to connect all the blocks.) Be sure to study the Setting Maps on page 71 and the various quilts showcased in the chapter. Position the squares one at a time on each corner of the sashing strip and sew diagonally corner to corner. Fold the square over the corner to create a triangle and press. Attach the remaining squares the same way.

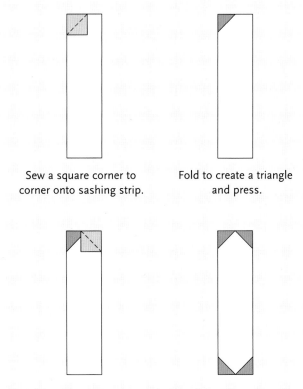

Sew a square corner to corner onto sashing strip.   Fold to create a triangle and press.

Attach remaining squares.

TIP: *When using this method, you can elect to leave the extra fabric layers or trim them away. Leaving them is easier and faster but adds to the bulk. The bulk can be a problem when it comes to quilting. Some quilters trim both layers away, while others might only trim one layer. Experiment and determine which method works best for you.*

on the sashing strip. To make the replacement triangles, cut two squares that are the finished triangle size plus ⁷/₈". Cut the squares in half diagonally and sew the resulting triangles to the four corners of the sashing strip. Press the seams toward the triangles.

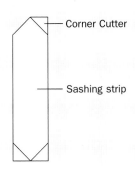
Use Corner Cutter to cut off the corners of the sashing strip.

Remove all the corners.

Cut replacement triangles.

Add replacement triangles to sashing strip.

1 Add ¹/₂" seam allowance plus ¹/₄" extra for insurance to 1 ¹/₄" and cut the framing strips at 2" wide. Sew them to all four sides of the original block.

2 Iron the block well and square it up to 12", raw edge to raw edge. (9" + 1 ¹/₄" + 1 ¹/₄" + ¹/₂" for seam allowances = 12".)

9" block

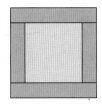
9" block with 2" strips

Framed block, trimmed to 12"

3 Cut 3" x 12" sashing strips. (2 ¹/₂" + ¹/₂" for seam allowances = 3" x size of block, raw edge to raw edge.)

Sashing strip cut size 3" x 12"

◆ To fit the $2\frac{1}{2}$" sashing, we would need $1\frac{1}{4}$" finished size replacement triangles.

If using the Corner Cutter technique, select the $1\frac{1}{4}$" Corner Cutter and eliminate the corners from the appropriate places on the sashing strip. The replacement triangle would be $1\frac{1}{4}$" + $\frac{7}{8}$" = $2\frac{1}{8}$" square, cut once, corner to corner.

1 1/4" Corner Cutter

Corner Cutter technique

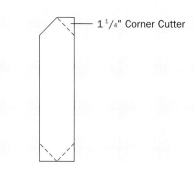

2 1/8" square cut once diagonally

If using the method of sewing a square corner to corner to the ends of the sashing strip, cut squares the finished triangle size plus $\frac{1}{2}$". For our finished $1\frac{1}{4}$" triangles, we would cut squares $1\frac{3}{4}$". Attach the squares as shown on page 68.

Setting the Blocks

You can set your blocks straight or on point and color the pieces any way you want. If the framing strips are the same color as the cornerstones and the triangles you attach to the sashing, you will create the Garden Maze illusion.

Star Flight
by Margret Reap, 51" x 51", 2002

Here are those blue Sawtooth Star blocks once again. Margret's color assignment was monochromatic. She had to work with blue and couldn't add any additional colors when setting her blocks. She set her blocks straight, but because the blocks were made by different quiltmakers, she knew she had to be able to reconcile size differential first. This setting is perfect for doing that. Just start with oversized strips for the initial framing when you need to reconcile size.

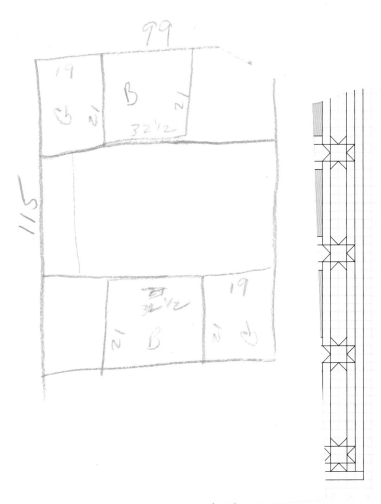

chapter. There is no rule that says how you must end the design. Each quiltmaker was free to choose the way her quilt would end. There are many decisions to be made— how wide to make your framing strips, how wide to make the sashing piece, how to color the pieces, how to end the pattern. There are no right or wrong answers but lots of personal favorites. Each quilt teaches us something different and gives us another way to look at the setting.

Setting Map for straight set

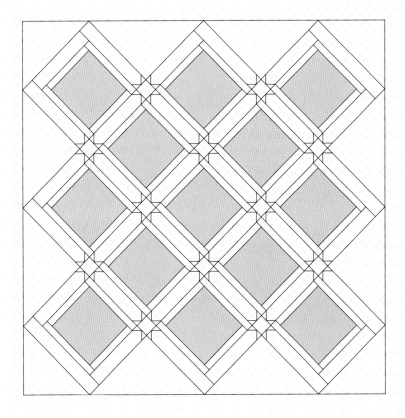

Setting Map for diagonal set

by Sharyn Craig, machine quilted by Joann Stuebing, 63" x 63", 2002

The green blocks you see in this quilt were part of a group exchange. You can also see them in *Pathway to the Stars* on page 74 where they have an Oriental feel with the addition of teal, black, and red, and in *Compromise* below where they turn warm, yellow, and spring-like. It's hard to believe all three quilts have the same green blocks—another example of how you can make any set of blocks into any color quilt.

Compromise

by Sharyn Craig, machine quilted by Joanie Keith, 68" x 68", 2001

In this quilt each block is framed with a different color strip. I wanted a scrappy recipe with colors that would lessen the intensity of some of those green blocks. I selected a warm yellow for the sashing pieces and the setting triangles and used a peach-tone fabric for the stars. I wanted subtle stars that the viewer had to look for, not stars that were the focal point. By piecing the setting triangles, I gave the illusion that the blocks were sitting on top of the borders. It's a very simple trick that adds a lot of visual interest.

y Assurance

⁄n Craig, machine quilted by Wendy
76" x 100", 2002

blocks for this quilt were inspired
quilt made by Marsha McCloskey
a book she co-authored with
Martin entitled *Pieced Borders:
Complete Resource.* I knew I
ted to use this Garden-Maze
ing and that I wanted to color it so
at the framing strips, triangles, and
ornerstones were all light value. I had
ighteen blocks to work with, which is
the perfect number for the diagonal
set. I could have used an additional
yellow strip at the outer edge of the
sashing pieces, but I didn't. I wanted
the Garden Maze to float, not "anchor."

Pathway to the Stars

by Laurine Leeke, 67" x 67", 2002

Laurine wanted to "lose the green" of her blocks and create a quilt with an Oriental feel. She chose black for the initial framing strips, a red print for both the sashing and the outer border, and many different teals for the stars. Notice the way she split some of her green blocks in half diagonally to use for the setting triangles. She did lose seam allowance and points by doing this, but personally I think it's a fantastic solution.

Patriotic Games

by Sharyn Craig, machine quilted by Laurie Daniels, 76" x 76", 2002

These blocks were given to me by Carolyn Smith, who received them in a friendship exchange. They were a variety of sizes, so my first goal was to add piecing where necessary to make the blocks each 9". Many of the block backgrounds were very white, so I certainly could have worked with true red, white, and blue, but I was concerned that the quilt wouldn't be very warm, and I wanted a warm, patriotic quilt. Using the gold for the initial frame and the sashing strips between the blocks achieved that warm feeling.

Garden Variety

by Connie Chunn, 23" x 23", 2002

Connie started the 3" blocks she used in this quilt in 1994, but they got put on the back burner in favor of other, more interesting projects. When I invited Connie to participate in this project, she went searching for blocks she already had in the house. In her quilt you definitely don't see the Garden-Maze setting. Her stars at the corners are there, but they are very subtle. This is a good example of not making everything predictable and expected. The more you add variations, the more interesting your quilt becomes.

Studying the pictures of the quilts in this chapter is a good way to determine how you might want to set your blocks, color your pieces, and end the outer edges. But they aren't the only possibilities. Feel free to experiment and explore for yourself how you want to set and color your blocks.

CHAPTER 8

Ring-Around-the-Block Set

"I love creating a frame around individual blocks."

SHARYN

Ring-Around-the-Block Set

I love creating a frame around individual blocks. These frames can equalize blocks that have different patterns and perk up blocks that are all the same. I've yet to find a block that doesn't work and look good in a frame. I call the frame in this chapter Ring-Around-the-Block.

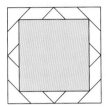

Simple Ring-Around-the-Block frame

What you see are simple parallelogram shapes, connected by a quarter-square triangle and finished off by half-square triangles in the corners.

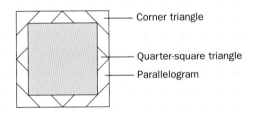

Corner triangle

Quarter-square triangle
Parallelogram

You can use these simple shapes in lots of different configurations and arrangements. You can frame the block straight or on point.

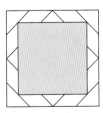

Block set straight

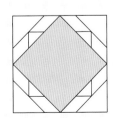

Block on point

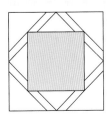

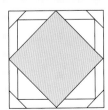

Ring-Around-the-Block variations

How to Design the Frame

I like to begin by drawing a square the size of my focus block on a piece of graph paper. I don't necessarily need to draw the actual focus block, but you can if you want to. You will need graph paper large enough for the full size block and the frame, so you may need to tape several sheets of graph paper together.

Next, I determine how I want to divide the space along one edge of the block. Depending on the finished size of your focus block, you can make the divisions equal or not. Let's begin with equal divisions.

1 For example, draw a 9" square on the paper. Divide 9 evenly by 3 into 3" increments. Put marks on the edge of the square every 3".

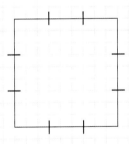

Put marks every 3".

2 The middle third is a quarter-square triangle. What you need to know about a quarter-square triangle is that its base is always twice its height. So if the base is 3", then the height is 1 1/2". Find the center of the 3" middle division. Measure exactly 1 1/2" up on the graph paper, and put a mark. Connect that mark to the ends of the middle division to create the center triangle.

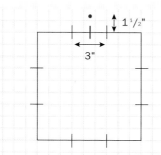

Mark 1 1/2" up from the square.

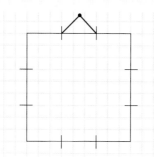

Connect the marks.

3 The distance from the base of the triangle to the corner of the original block is the size of the parallelogram's base. You will use this same measurement for the top line of the parallelogram. Starting from the point of the triangle, measure in each direction that same amount and put a mark.

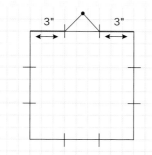

Measure the parallelogram's base.

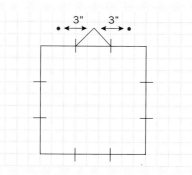

Measure and put marks.

4 Connect the marks and you have the diagram for the Ring-Around-the-Block pieces.

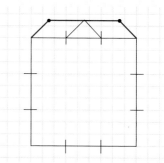

Connect the marks.

5 If you want the block to sit straight in this frame, the side edge of the corner half-square triangle will be twice the height of the quarter-square triangle. If you want the corner triangles to turn your block on point, then the corner triangle will be the same length as the 2 parallelograms that it touches.

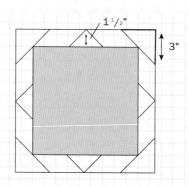

Triangles on straight set block, side of triangle is twice the height of the quarter-square triangle.

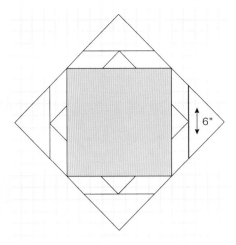

Triangles on-point set block, base of triangle is equal to 2 parallelograms.

When designing, start with the triangle in the middle. It needs to be centered on the edge of the focus block, but it does not need to be one-third of the block. If your original block was 10" you might have a 4" quarter-square triangle and parallelograms that are 3" on the long edges.

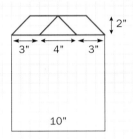

10" block variation

Another example might be an 8" focus block with a 4" quarter-square triangle in the middle. That would leave 2" for the edges of the parallelograms.

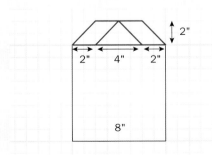

8" focus block variation

Cutting the Pieces and Making the Block

1 You could easily cut the quarter-square triangle using rotary math numbers. Add 1 $^1/_4$" to the measurement of the long edge of the triangle. Cut a square that size and cut twice from corner to corner. Each square will yield the 4 triangles that you need to frame each block.

Example: Using a 9" block with equal divisions, you will need a 3" quarter-square triangle. 3" + 1 $^1/_4$" = 4 $^1/_4$" square to be cut twice corner to corner.

Long side of triangle + 1$^1/_4$"

Cut twice diagonally for center triangle.

2 For the parallelograms, add $^1/_4$" seam allowances to all 4 sides of your drawn parallelogram and make a template. Cut a fabric strip equal to the height of the parallelogram template. Position the template on the fabric strip and cut. Using the template material described on page 111, you have a rotary friendly template that you can't destroy with your rotary cutter. You will need 8 parallelograms to frame each block.

Add $^1/_4$" seam allowances to parallelogram.

Place template on fabric strip and cut.

TIP: Remember that parallelograms are directional pieces. You need one right-facing and one left-facing parallelogram to create your frame. If you position your template on a strip that is folded wrong sides together, you can cut your parallelograms and they will automatically have the mirror-image shapes you need.

3 For corner triangles that will keep the block straight in the frame, you will need half-square triangles. Add ⁷⁄₈" to the finished triangle size to give you the size of square to cut. Cut squares that size, then cut each square once from corner to corner. You will need 2 squares to make 4 triangles to frame each block.

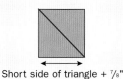

Short side of triangle + ⁷⁄₈"

Cut once diagonally for corner triangle.

4 If you want your block on point in the frame, determining the size of the triangle can take a bit more math, but it is not difficult. To avoid the math altogether, you can elect to make a template for this piece by adding ¹⁄₄" seam allowances to all the edges of the finished triangle and creating a template. Position the template on the fabric so the straight of grain will fall on the short sides of the triangle.

Position triangle template on a strip of fabric to give you straight of grain on the 2 short sides.

If you prefer to cut the triangles without templates, then divide the long base of the triangle by 1.414. This will give you the size of the short side of the triangle. Add ⁷⁄₈" to that number to obtain the size of square you will need to cut. Cut a square, then cut it once corner to corner. By doing this, you will have the straight of grain where you want it—along the outside edge of the block.

Example: 6" base length ÷ 1.414 = 4.2433" + .875" (⁷⁄₈" in decimals) = 5.1183"...or close enough to 5¹⁄₈" for most of us quilters!

5 To make the frame, sew a parallelogram to either side of each center quarter-square triangle. Make four parallelogram/triangle units for each block and sew to the sides of the block. Press and add the 4 corner triangles. Iron well.

TIP: *You can frame any size block, but this frame works best with blocks that are all the same size. This may mean you need to reconcile size differential before you can start designing your ring frame. Your size problem can be resolved with simple framing strips or triangles.*

More Ideas

Study the quilts presented in this chapter and read the information about each one. You'll pick up some handy tips and tricks by reading what the quiltmakers did to make their focus blocks easy to deal with. You will also find more examples in the Gallery of Quilts on page 86.

Basically Blue

by Sharyn Craig, machine quilted by Phyllis
Reddish, 44" x 54", 2002

My color assignment for these
Sawtooth Star blocks was teal and
purple. Because the original star
block is a four-patch, I divided the
ring frame the same way, making the
triangle a 3" quarter-square triangle.
The parallelograms are $1\frac{1}{2}$" on the
short sides, and the corner triangles
are 3" half-square triangles. The height
of the parallelograms makes the
frame appear more pointed and not
as circular as many of the other quilts
you'll see in this chapter.

Christmas on the Farm

by Linda Packer, 60" x 60", 2000

Linda did some really fun things
with her frame to give the viewer
even more to look at. Instead of plain
triangles in the corners, she pieced
them with one square and two triangles
per corner. Next she continued the
edge of the parallelogram into the
border. To best appreciate what the
quiltmakers did, you need to be able
to view each block independently,
while at the same time you want a
quilt that is unified. Linda achieved
these two goals beautifully.

Tea Party

by Sharyn Craig, machine quilted by Joanie
Keith, 58" x 58", 2001

I've often thought that good things
are worth waiting for, and this quilt
is a perfect example. In 1997 when
I exchanged these blocks, I had
absolutely no idea how I wanted to
work with them. I put them in a box
on a shelf, figuring that I'd deal with
this problem tomorrow. When I finally
got them out to work with, I knew I
needed to provide space for each
block to be seen. Because they were
extremely diverse in theme, color,
and most importantly, size, I used
many of the size reconciliation
techniques discussed in Chapter 1 to
fix those problems.

ADVICE FROM SHARYN:

*Maybe some of you have had a
set of blocks that you didn't have
a clue what to do with. For some
quiltmakers, putting these blocks
on a closet shelf is like the "kiss
of death." They're sure they'll never
see them again. But I look at
these blocks like good cheese or
wine. I figure that they need time
to age before they are really at
their prime.*

Antigua, Me Come From

by Marnie Santos, 72" x 65", 2002

Marnie made this quilt for a great niece who had been born in Antigua. During a visit, the niece and Marnie visited a local quilt shop and the niece bought lots of fabric for Marnie as a thank you for her delightful hospitality. Marnie decided to use the fabric to make a special quilt for her niece to celebrate their relationship. She made blocks that had special ties to Antigua. Since this is a sampler quilt loaded with lots of visual stimulation, the frame became a calming statement for the blocks.

Summer's Song

by Louise Hixon, 56" x 56", 2002

This quilt and the one that follows use the exact same blocks as *Primarily Primary* on page 21, *Confetti* on page 93, and *Lemon Drops* on page 94. In this quilt Louise took some very bright blocks and made a primarily blue and yellow quilt. She used the Ring-Around-the-Block frame, but once again altered the corners like we've seen in a few other quilts. She colored the corners with alternate blue and yellow squares, which created that fun little four-patch where the blocks come together.

Same Song Second Verse
by Louise Hixon, 57" x 57", 2002

I love the overall visual softness of this quilt, in spite of the intensity of the colors in the original blocks. Louise machine appliquéd the soft yellow flowers in the diagonal rows to add a wonderful, delicate look. This quilt definitely fits into the definition of a successful quilt...one that you see the whole quilt first, then your eye is drawn back again and again to see what special things the quiltmaker has done in the creation of this quilt.

Redwork Santas
by Sandra Munsey, 60" x 60", 2001

Sandra embroidered these nine Santa designs using a Kari Pearson pattern and was looking for a way to frame each block independently. She wanted to create a quilt with a homespun feeling, so she selected the red and white plaids for the frame pieces.

" My redwork Santas needed a lively frame. Ring-Around-the-Block using plaids gave the blocks the needed spark. This set introduced me to a new way of looking at pieced blocks as a resource for more interesting frames for my redwork and appliqué blocks. "

Sandra Munsey, Forestdale, Massachusetts

Plaid Peonies

by Mary Pavlovich, machine quilted by Quality Quilting in Stover, MO, 60" x 60", 2002

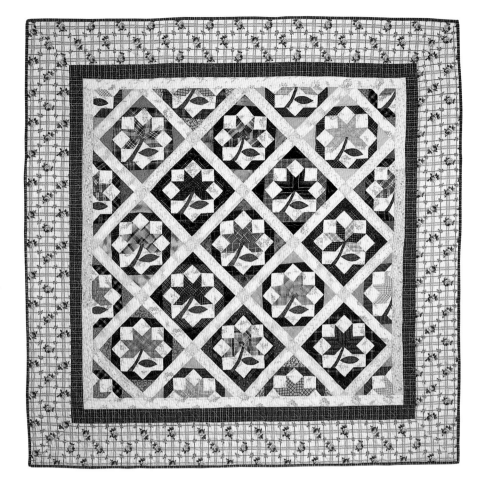

Mary started the Peony blocks in a workshop I taught several years ago. She enjoyed making the blocks so much that she just kept going and going. Finally she realized it was time to stop making blocks and begin designing the quilt!

I love the way Mary deliberately sliced her blocks to create the setting triangles. She framed them, then took the rotary cutter and whacked away. This is a fun and unique solution for handling setting triangles.

So now that you've looked at some great examples, what's your plan? First, look at your blocks. Next, think about color potential. Get out that graph paper, and let's give this setting a try. I know you'll like the results.

CHAPTER 9

Gallery of Quilts

*"Use these
images to
further stimulate
your own
creative juices."*
SHARYN

Gallery of Quilts

Inspired by the Seven Settings

he purpose of this chapter is to showcase quilts that didn't fit neatly into any one of the individual setting chapters. The quiltmakers may have borrowed from the various chapters and incorporated the concepts into the quilt, or they may just have been inspired by something that they saw. If the interpretation was not obvious enough to have been shared in the specific chapter, I hope you'll enjoy the visual stimulation of seeing it here in the gallery. Use these images to further stimulate your own creative juices.

I know that when you start out using a book like this, you feel much more comfortable sticking to the original recipes and Setting Maps you encountered in the individual chapters. If you go back through the book, you'll see that's what most of the quilters have done. Then after you've "colored inside the lines" long enough, you might want to experiment and try something a little bit different.

If you want a purple Christmas quilt, then do it. You don't have to please anyone but yourself with these quilts you're making. Quilting is supposed to be fun and fulfilling. I love to think of my quilts as my legacy to my family. Through my books I hope I can help you achieve the type of quilts you want to leave to your family.

If my quilts are the legacy for my children and grandchildren, then I hope my books are the legacy I'm creating for quilters today. I also hope that what you take away from this book inspires you with enthusiasm to make individually creative quilts and to get some of those leftover, ongoing, orphan-like blocks out of closets and into finished quilts.

Spumoni Sorbet

by Sharyn Craig, machine quilted by Phyllis Reddish, 60" x 83", 2002

Have you ever participated in an Orphan Block Swap? Imagine everyone showing up with blocks they don't want any more. Each person puts their orphan blocks on the floor in the center of the room. Other people are encouraged to "adopt" someone else's orphan blocks to take home and work with. That's where I got this set of blocks made years earlier by Margaret Reap. This quilt combines the Two-for-One and Ring-Around-the-Block maps.

Forget Me Not

by Carolyn Smith, 78" x 78", 2002

Believe it or not, it was the Chain Set that inspired Carolyn to create this quilt. Even though there is no alternating Chain block, she was still able to create the illusion of squares connecting the star blocks. Yes, these are the same blue stars that we've seen all the way through the book. She was trying to create the feeling of a French country bedroom and chose several large chintz-like floral fabrics to use with her blocks. She framed each of the star blocks first with a stripe, then a floral with the blue squares in the corners.

Stars Plus

by Laurine Leeke, 52" x 52", 2002

The Windblown-Square Set inspired Laurine this time. Yet, while many of the visual images are similar to the quilts you saw in Chapter 3, the blocks were not created in the same manner. She actually created the quilt by sewing light triangles onto some of the blue stars and dark (red and blue) triangles onto other stars. These framed blocks were set on point. Her patriotic color scheme was created by adding red to the blue star blocks.

Memory Bouquet

by Laurine Leeke, quilted by Wendy Knight, 62" x 65", 2002

The Nosegay blocks were made in a Doreen Speckman workshop in the mid 1990s, and the floral appliqué blocks were given to Laurine by a friend. When Laurine first showed me the very red appliqué blocks and the very pastel Nosegay blocks, I was quite skeptical that she could actually combine them successfully into one quilt. Her solution is wonderful and has a little bit of everything: coping triangles, coping strips, remade blocks, and trimmed-down blocks. She was obviously inspired by the concepts in the book but not bound by anything she'd ever seen before.

Alaskan Souvenir

by Marnie Santos, 62" x 62", 2002

Marnie purchased the Matryoshka doll fabric in Sitka, Alaska. Like any impulse buy that you can't go back and get more of, the fabric presented Marnie with lots of challenges. Because it was directional, it was very difficult to just randomly cut. The fact that she had a limited amount of it, and could get no more, made for an even greater challenge. Her favorite palette is scrappy with lots of different fabrics, but this time she limited herself to only a few additional fabrics. She opted for the Crossover Set with varying-width pointy pieces.

Confetti

by Lynn Johnson, machine quilted by Wendy Knight, 71" x 71", 2002

Lynn was inspired by the Chain Set. "Confetti" is the perfect name for this quilt. When I see this quilt, I can just imagine scraps of fabric being thrown into the air and fluttering down. Her playful use of color in the Chain blocks and into the side setting triangles reinforces the scrappy images that bring the focus blocks together cohesively. Strategic piecing in the setting triangles also keeps the viewer guessing about how this quilt was constructed.

Lemon Drops

by Lynn Johnson, machine quilted by Wendy Knight, 65" x 81", 2002

Confetti and *Lemon Drops* used the same original focus blocks. This time Lynn used more of the intense colors of the original blocks. She was inspired by the Windblown Square but eliminated one whole set of the first frame triangles. She framed her original blocks with coping strips in a light-value fabric, then alternated the pieced blocks with simple Pinwheel blocks. The blocks were all put on point with pieced setting triangles.

Barely Christmas

by Margret Reap, 68" x 68", 2002

I love this quilt and honestly had a lot of trouble deciding where to include it. Margret began with some simple Sawtooth Stars. She framed them with Ring-Around-the-Block, then set the framed block into the Garden-Maze sashing. You definitely do not see the Garden Maze because of the wide light strips that frame each block. Margret also has very subtle red stars at the four inside intersections. Another fun touch was meander cutting the edge of the quilt, after quilting and before binding. I love the concept and feel it's perfect for this quilt.

The Perfect Age

by Margret Reap, 59" x 59", 2002

How perfect that the final quilt in the book should be yet another blue star quilt. Margret chose a Square-in-a-Square Set, framed to give the chain effect for the alternating block to the stars, with framing triangles composed of quarter-Crossover blocks. This quilt definitely sums up so much of what I've been saying all the way through the book. I want you to use what you've learned from me in this book to create your own individual, unique quilts.

CHAPTER 10

Blocks, Charts & Helpful Hints

"There are
only four basic
pattern shapes
in the blocks
I've selected."

SHARYN

or those of you who don't have a stockpile of blocks, or those of you who would rather start a new project than work with what you have on hand, these blocks are for you. Many of the blocks I included are present in one or more of the quilts in this book. I chose some of the other blocks just because I liked them. All were picked because they can be cut easily using rotary numbers. A total of fourteen pattern pieces are needed to create all of these blocks. The pieces are numbered so that whenever you see a #1 pattern piece, it is exactly the same size as a #1 pattern piece in a different block. This explains why the numbers on any one block may not be in sequential order.

You may choose to cut your pieces with the rotary numbers, or if you prefer to work with templates, you can use the numbers to create templates for the blocks. The choice is up to you.

 TIP: *If you're a template person, refer to page 111 for information on a product I heartily recommend for making templates, John Flynn's Cut Your Own Template Kit.*

It's common knowledge that many blocks have multiple names. Also some block names have different images. Some blocks were chosen from quilts I saw pictured in magazines, in books, or at quilt shows. The name assigned to the quilt had absolutely nothing to do with the particular block. In instances where it was a block I was not familiar with, I literally made up a name for the block. So don't be surprised if you don't agree with a name you see by a block. Think of the names as merely reference tools.

I've included a cutting guide for both a 6" and 9" block. The common symbols indicate what shape you need to cut, and the numbers beside the symbols are for the cut size of each piece, which means they include the seam allowance.

Common symbols for rotary cutting

Square	Rectangle	Half-square triangle	Quarter-square triangle

Blocks

Sawtooth Star

Carolyn's Star

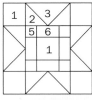
Quiltmaker's Star

Dutchman's Puzzle

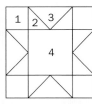
Grandmother's Favorite

Fox and Geese

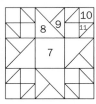
Churn Dash

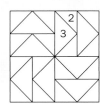
Weathervane

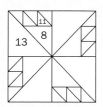

Rosebud

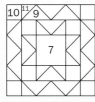

Union Square

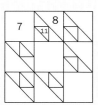

Cat's Cradle

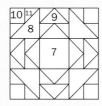

Eddystone Light

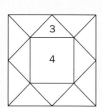

Windblown Square

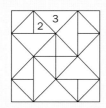

Puss in the Corner

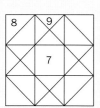

Swamp Angel

Mosaic #11

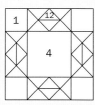

Square in a Star

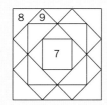

Gentleman's Fancy

Pieces

Piece Number		Size for 6" block		Size for 9" block	
1	☐	$1^1/_2$"	(2")	$2^1/_4$"	($2^3/_4$")
2	◻	$1^1/_2$"	($2^3/_8$")	$2^1/_4$"	($3^1/_8$")
3	⊠	3"	($4^1/_4$")	$4^1/_2$"	($5^3/_4$")
4	☐	3"	($3^1/_2$")	$4^1/_2$"	(5")
5	☐	$^3/_4$"	($1^1/_4$")	$1^1/_8$"	($1^5/_8$")
6	☐	$^3/_4$"	($1^1/_4$")	$1^1/_8$"	($1^5/_8$")
		$1^1/_2$"	(2")	$2^1/_4$"	($2^3/_4$")
7	☐	2"	($2^1/_2$")	3"	($3^1/_2$")
8	◻	2"	($2^7/_8$")	3"	($3^7/_8$")
9	⊠	2"	($3^1/_4$")	3"	($4^1/_4$")
10	☐	1"	($1^1/_2$")	$1^1/_2$"	(2")
11	◻	1"	($1^7/_8$")	$1^1/_2$"	($2^3/_8$")
12	⊠	$1^1/_2$"	($2^3/_4$")	$2^1/_4$"	($3^1/_2$")
13	◻	3"	($3^7/_8$")	$4^1/_2$"	($5^3/_8$")
14	☐	1"	($1^1/_2$")	$1^1/_2$"	(2")
		2"	($2^1/_2$")	3"	($3^1/_2$")

NOTE: The number in parentheses is the cutting number, including seam allowance.

Pattern Piece Basics

There are only four basic pattern shapes in the blocks I've selected. Those shapes are the square, rectangle, half-square triangle, and the quarter-square triangle. Each of those shapes has a common symbol that I illustrated on page 98. I have told you exactly how big to cut each piece in the blocks based on the finished 6" and 9" sizes. Someday you might want to make your blocks a different size. You might need to know how to cut these shapes in other sizes. This is what you need to know:

Square: To cut a square with the rotary cutter and no template, you take the finished size of the square and add $1/2$".

Example: A 4" square would be cut $4\,1/2$" x $4\,1/2$".

Rectangle: To cut a rectangle without a template, you take the finished measurement of the sides and add $1/2$" to each side.

Example: A 2" x 4" rectangle would be cut $2\,1/2$" by $4\,1/2$".

Half-square triangle: These triangles are literally half of a square, which is why the cutting symbol is a square with the diagonal line drawn once, corner to corner.

Symbol for the half-square triangle cutting guide

To cut a half-square triangle, you take the finished measurement of the short side of the triangle and add $7/8$". Cut a square this new size and cut it once corner to corner.

Example: A 4" half-square triangle would be cut from a $4\,7/8$" square, cut once corner to corner.

Quarter-square triangle: It takes four of these triangles to equal one square, which is why the cutting symbol is a square with diagonal lines drawn twice, from corner to corner.

Symbol for the quarter-square triangle cutting guide

To cut a quarter-square triangle, you take the finished size of the long side of the triangle and add $1\,1/4$". The long side of the triangle is the same as the side of the square. Look at the diagram to confirm this concept.

Example: A 4" quarter-square triangle would be cut from a $5\,1/4$" square, cut twice corner to corner.

It is nice to know the math involved so you can cut any triangle any size you want without having to rely on someone else's decision for block size. You might not want to make your blocks either 6" or 9". You might want to make your blocks 12". Won't it be nice to know how to convert the numbers for yourself?

On the other hand, some of you just like to be given the answers. I am providing you with an easy-to-read chart for cutting both half and quarter-square triangles in a variety of common sizes.

Chart for Cutting Half- and Quarter-Square Triangles

Finished size	Cut size for	Cut size for
1"	1 7/8"	2 1/4"
1 1/2"	2 3/8"	2 3/4"
2"	2 7/8"	3 1/4"
2 1/2"	3 3/8"	3 3/4"
3"	3 7/8"	4 1/4"
3 1/2"	4 3/8"	4 3/4"
4"	4 7/8"	5 1/4"
4 1/2"	5 3/8"	5 3/4"
5"	5 7/8"	6 1/4"
5 1/2"	6 3/8"	6 3/4"
6"	6 7/8"	7 1/4"
6 1/2"	7 3/8"	7 3/4"
7"	7 7/8"	8 1/4"
7 1/2"	8 3/8"	8 3/4"
8"	8 7/8"	9 1/4"
8 1/2"	9 3/8"	9 3/4"
9"	9 7/8"	10 1/4"
9 1/2"	10 3/8"	10 3/4"
10"	10 7/8"	11 1/4"
10 1/2"	11 3/8"	11 3/4"

When calculating sizes, always work in finished numbers, then add the seam allowances. Keeping the numbers straight, however, can be a problem. When making notes for myself, I put parentheses around the cutting numbers. That way I know instantly whether I'm looking at finished sizes or cutting sizes.

TIP: *I put the parentheses around cutting numbers when I'm writing as a safeguard against cutting the wrong sizes.*

Example: 1" = finished size   (1 1/2") = cut size

Many quilters get confused about whether they are working with cut or finished sizes and numbers. When we refer to block sizes, we always refer to finished sizes. We would never say, "I made a 12 1/2" block" when, in fact, the finished block size is 12". We would refer to the block as a 12" block.

TIP: *When I draw the symbol for the half-square triangle, I write the size to the left of the triangle. When drawing the symbol for the quarter-square triangle, I mark the size under the long edge. Being consistent about the way you mark your symbols helps to prevent cutting errors later.*

Number position for marking the half- and quarter-square triangles

Diagonally Set Quilts

If you opt to set your blocks on point, you need to fill in the edges with what are called setting triangles. There are side setting triangles and corner setting triangles.

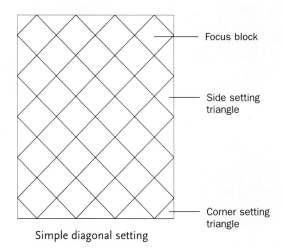

Simple diagonal setting

Determining Size of Setting Triangles for Simple Diagonal Setting

To calculate the cutting measurement for these triangles you need to first recognize that you will want the straight of grain along the outside edge of the quilt.

Side Setting Triangles

To cut the side setting triangles with the straight of grain on the long edge, you need to first learn the measurement of the long edge of these triangles.

NOTE: In our illustration for the Simple Diagonal Set, the blocks are touching, without sashing, therefore the short side of the finished side setting triangles is exactly the same as the finished size of the blocks.

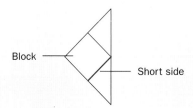

Short side of the finished triangle = finished size of the blocks.

① To determine the size of the long side, take the finished size of the short side of the triangle and multiply times 1.414.

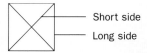

Finished short side x 1.414 = finished long side.

② To determine the size square you need to cut, add 1 ¹/₄" to that amount. Cut the square twice corner to corner for the cut triangles.

Cut square into 4 triangles.

Example: Based on 9" finished focus blocks:

9" x 1.414 = 12.73" (long side of side setting triangle)

12.73" + 1.25" = 13.98", or in quilter's language, 14" (size of square to cut for side setting triangles).

Cut a 14" square and cut twice corner to corner.

When working in decimals, if it doesn't come out an exact nice number, you want to round up to the nearest eighth of an inch. Refer to the decimal equivalent chart on page 108 for help in converting decimals to the fractions we are used to working with.

Corner Setting Triangles

Looking at our quilt illustration again, you can see that the long edge of the corner setting triangle matches the side of the focus block.

The corner setting triangle needs to be cut as a half-square triangle so that straight of grain falls on the edge of the quilt. To create a half-square triangle, you need to determine the short side of the triangle.

1 To determine the size of the short side, take the finished size of the long side of the triangle and divide by 1.414.

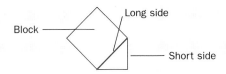

Finished long side ÷ 1.414 = finished short side

2 To determine the size square you need to cut, add $^7/_8$" to that amount. Cut the square once corner to corner for the cut triangles.

Cut square into 2 triangles.

Example: Again using the 9" finished focus block: 9" ÷ 1.414 = 6.36" (short side of corner setting triangles).

6.36" + .875" = 7.24", or in quilter's language, 7 $^1/_4$" (size of square to cut for corner setting triangles).

Cut a 7 $^1/_4$" square and cut once corner to corner.

Determining Size of Setting Triangles for Diagonal Setting with Sashing

Including sashing into the setting of the blocks changes the numbers.

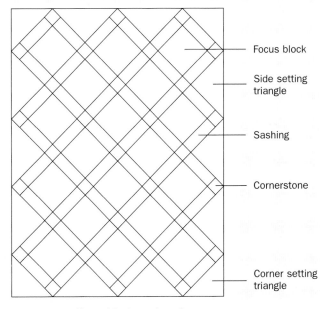

Diagonally set blocks with sashing

You will notice that the short side of the side setting triangles is equal to the side of a block plus the width of the sashing. You must add the finished width of the sashing to the finished width of the block to find the short side of the side setting triangles. You will notice that the long side of the corner setting triangles is equal to the side of a block plus the finished width of two strips of sashing because there is a sashing strip on each side of the block.

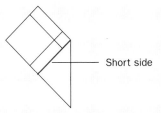

Short side of side setting triangle = side of block + sashing.

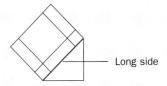

Long side of corner setting triangle = side of block + 2 strips of sashing.

Example: Based on 9" finished focus blocks with 2" finished sashing strips:

Side Setting Triangles:
9" + 2" = 11" (short side of side setting triangles), 11" x 1.414 = 15.55" (long side of side setting triangles), 15.55" + 1.25" = 16.80", or 16 $7/8$" in quilter's language (size of square to cut for side setting triangles).

Cut a 16 $7/8$" square, cut it twice corner to corner to yield the side setting triangles.

Corner Setting Triangles:
9" + 2" + 2" = 13" (long side of corner setting triangles),
13" ÷ 1.414 = 9.19" (short side of corner setting triangles),
9.19" + .875" = 10.06" (size of square to cut for corner setting triangles).

In this instance I would cut a slightly "healthy" 10" square and cut once corner to corner to get the corner setting triangles. If you're more comfortable cutting 10 $1/8$" rather than assuming you're being generous enough with a "healthy" 10", then that's fine. It's always possible to trim the edges down if you cut these triangles too large, but it can be a real problem if you cut them too small.

If you would rather not have to go through all this, you can use the setting triangle chart. It is always good to know how to calculate these triangles in case some day you want to make a block size not found on the chart. Remember, you always round up to the nearest $1/8$" when in doubt.

Rotary Cutting Numbers for Side and Corner Setting Triangles

Block or Block-Plus Sashing Size	Square Size to Cut for Side Triangles ⊠	Square Size to Cut for Corner Triangles ◺
6"	9 $3/4$"	5 $1/8$"
6 $1/2$"	10 $1/2$"	5 $1/2$"
7"	11 $1/4$"	5 $7/8$"
7 $1/2$"	11 $7/8$"	6 $1/4$"
8"	12 $5/8$"	6 $5/8$"
8 $1/2$"	13 $3/8$"	7"
9"	14"	7 $1/4$"
9 $1/2$"	14 $3/4$"	7 $5/8$"
10"	15 $1/2$"	8"
10 $1/2$"	16 $1/8$"	8 $3/8$"
11"	16 $7/8$"	8 $3/4$"
11 $1/2$"	17 $5/8$"	9"
12"	18 $1/4$"	9 $3/8$"
12 $1/2$"	19"	9 $3/4$"
13"	19 $3/4$"	10 $1/8$"
13 $1/2$"	20 $3/8$"	10 $1/2$"
14"	21 $1/8$"	10 $7/8$"
14 $1/2$"	21 $3/4$"	11 $1/8$"
15"	22 $1/2$"	11 $1/2$"
15 $1/2$"	23 $1/4$"	11 $7/8$"
16"	23 $7/8$"	12 $1/4$"
16 $1/2$"	24 $5/8$"	12 $5/8$"
17"	25 $3/8$"	13"
17 $1/2$"	26"	13 $1/4$"
18"	26 $3/4$"	13 $5/8$"
18 $1/2$"	27 $1/2$"	14"

Calculating the Diagonal of a Square

When you set the blocks on point, it is helpful to know how big that is going to make your quilt. The math to make this calculation is the same as you used to find the long edge of the side setting triangle: Finished size of block x 1.414 = finished diagonal measurement of the block.

Example: 6" block set on point:

6" x 1.414 = 8.48", or 8 1/2" to quilters, (diagonal measurement of the block).

If you were setting your blocks 4 across by 6 down, you would calculate the size of your quilt by multiplying 4 x 8 1/2"= 34" (width of quilt), and 6 x 8 1/2" = 51" (finished length of quilt).

You can do your own the calculations, or use the chart below.

Diagonal measurement of squares

Size of Finished Square	Diagonal Measurement
6"	8 1/2"
7"	9 7/8"
8"	11 3/8"
9"	12 3/4"
10"	14 1/8"
11"	15 1/2"
12"	17"
13"	18 3/8"
14"	19 7/8"
15"	21 1/4"
16"	22 5/8"

Corner Triangles for Square-in-a-Square

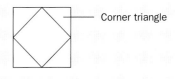
Corner triangle

Square-in-a-Square

The triangles used to frame a block such as you need for Coping Triangles, Square-in-a-Square Set, and the Two-for-One Set would be calculated exactly the same as the corner setting triangles in a diagonally set quilt. The finished long side of a corner framing triangle is equal to the finished size of the block you are framing. Since you need the finished size of the short side to get straight of grain on the outer edges, take the finished block size and divide by 1.414. Add 7/8" to determine the size square to cut, and then cut once diagonally.

Example: 6" finished block:

6" ÷ 1.414 = 4.24" (finished short side of the triangle) + .875" = 5.118"(size of cut square), 5 1/8" in quilter's language.

Cut the 5 1/8" square once corner to corner for your triangles.

Here's a simple chart provided for you to use for some of the common block sizes.

Corner Triangle Sizes for Square-in-a-Square

Finished Block Size	Size Square to Cut
6"	$5\,^1/_8$"
7"	$5\,^7/_8$"
8"	$6\,^5/_8$"
9"	$7\,^1/_4$"
10"	8"
11"	$8\,^3/_4$"
12"	$9\,^3/_8$"

Corner Cutter Guides

A term used frequently throughout the chapters is Corner Cutter. Corner Cutters give you an easy way to eliminate the corner from a shape. They were used to create the Garden Maze setting and to modify some of the blocks in the Square-in-a-Square. Corner Cutters were also used to modify coping triangles in several quilts in the Gallery, as well as in the Two-for-One Set chapter.

In a nutshell this is what you need to know to create a Corner Cutter guide:

Finished size of triangle you want to cut away PLUS $^1/_8$".

To create this Corner Cutter guide, I would use eight-to-the-inch graph paper and draw two lines perpendicular to one another (in an "L" shape) equal to the finished size of the triangle plus the $^1/_8$". Let's use a 3" finished triangle for our example. Draw two lines $3\,^1/_8$" at right angles to one another. Next connect the opposite ends of the lines.

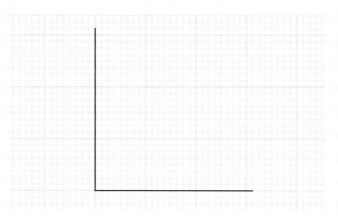

Draw two lines, each $3\,^1/_8$" long at right angles to each other.

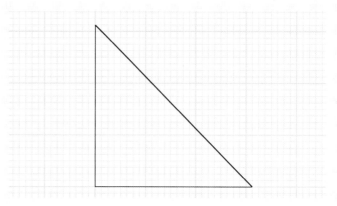

Connect the ends of the lines to make a 3" Corner Cutter.

To use this guide, I would cut it out and either tape it to the underside of the rotary ruler with the long edge of the guide along the edge of the ruler, or I would make a sturdy independent template with the John Flynn template material. Position the square corner of the guide at the corner you wish to eliminate, and trim.

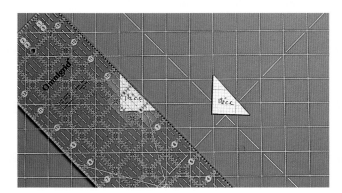

Template taped to underside of rotary ruler and independent guide

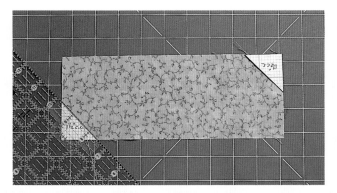

Using the Corner Cutter guide to trim shapes

Or you can prepare a ruler specifically for Corner Cutters. When I made mine I went to a Plexiglas supply house and purchased a 6" square. I used a glue stick to adhere the guides to the underneath side of the 6" square. To protect the guides I positioned a piece of clear Contact® paper over the paper guides. If you prefer the individual guides, you might want to make several of them and keep a box of the most popular sized Corner Cutter templates ready by your cutting table for any time you need them. Having them there means you are more likely to use them when the need arises.

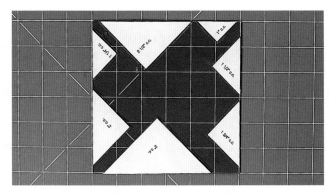

Corner Cutter ruler created by gluing guides to a 6" square of Plexiglas

For your convenience I'm sharing some of my favorite sizes. If you have the guides photocopied so you can cut them out to use, be sure to request that they be copied at 100%. What you don't need is to have them be inaccurate because you didn't realize the importance of requesting the 100% factor.

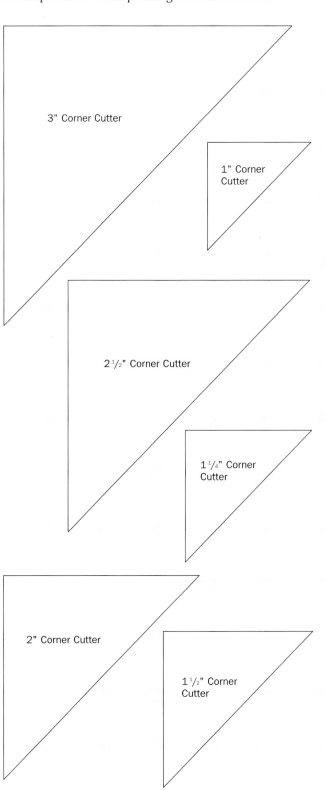

Corner Cutter template guides

Replacement Triangles for the Corner Cutters

In situations like the Garden-Maze setting, once you've eliminated the corners from the sashing strips you need to reattach new triangles. The replacement triangles are half-square triangles. You would use the same math as discussed earlier under the part about the half-square triangles. So a 3" replacement triangle would be cut from a $3\frac{7}{8}$" square, cut once corner to corner. You can use the exact same chart for these triangles as provided for the half-square triangles.

More Charts

Decimal Equivalency Chart

Decimal	Fraction Equivalent
.0625	$\frac{1}{16}$
.125	$\frac{1}{8}$
.1666	$\frac{1}{6}$
.1875	$\frac{3}{16}$
.25	$\frac{1}{4}$
.3125	$\frac{5}{16}$
.3333	$\frac{1}{3}$
.375	$\frac{3}{8}$
.4375	$\frac{7}{16}$
.5	$\frac{1}{2}$
.5625	$\frac{9}{16}$
.625	$\frac{5}{8}$
.6666	$\frac{2}{3}$
.6875	$\frac{11}{16}$
.75	$\frac{3}{4}$
.8125	$\frac{13}{16}$
.833	$\frac{5}{6}$
.875	$\frac{7}{8}$
.9375	$\frac{15}{16}$

Number of Sashings and Cornerstones Needed for Straight Set Blocks

Total Number of Blocks	Number of Blocks Across	Number of Blocks Down	Number of Sashing Pieces for Internal Only	Number of Sashing Pieces for Internal and External	Number of Cornerstones for Internal Only	Number of Cornerstones for Internal and External
9	3	3	12	24	4	16
12	3	4	17	31	6	20
15	3	5	22	38	8	24
16	4	4	24	40	9	25
20	4	5	31	49	12	30
25	5	5	40	60	16	36
24	4	6	38	58	15	35
30	5	6	49	71	20	42
35	5	7	58	82	24	48

Sashing, Cornerstones, Side Triangles, and Corner Triangles for Diagonal Set Blocks

Number of Blocks Across	Number of Blocks Down	Total Number of Blocks	Number of Sashing Pieces	Number of Cornerstones	Number of Side Triangles	Number of Corner Triangles
2	2	5	16	12	4	4
2	3	8	24	17	6	4
3	3	13	36	24	8	4
3	4	18	48	31	10	4
4	4	25	64	40	12	4
4	5	32	80	49	14	4

Glossary of Terms

Audition. When I let fabric or a block "try out" for placement in my quilt, I refer to that process as an audition. A block can be auditioned on the flannel wall, with paper and pencil, or even through your computer if that's your thing.

Color Correction. This is a term I use when I am either not happy with the colors of the original blocks, or I just want to make a quilt that is different from those colors present in the blocks. I alter the colors by adding ones to the equation that weren't in the blocks to begin with.

Coping Strips. These are oversized framing bands of fabric sewn to the edges of the blocks to change their size or color before squaring them up. The coping strips can be attached to any number of edges on the blocks. They do not have to totally frame the block.

Coping Triangles. Like coping strips, these are oversized triangle-shaped pieces of fabric sewn to the four edges of the block before squaring to change the size of the block or enhance the color.

Cornerstones. These are small squares of fabric positioned at the intersections between sashing strips. Usually they are cut from a fabric that contrasts to the sashing fabric.

Finger pressing. During construction of a block, I recommend this process of pressing. Run the underneath edge of your thumbnail along the seam edge from the right side of the pieces to give it a crisp edge. There may be some stretching, but the pieces will recover their original shape since no heat has been applied. Wait until the block is completed to iron.

Flannel wall. This is also known as a design wall. It is often white cotton flannel, or cotton batting, fixed to a firm surface. Blocks and fabric adhere to it. It is very useful during the design phase to position blocks and move them around when you are looking for just the right arrangement.

Focus blocks. These are the blocks you need to set together into a quilt. They can be pieced, appliquéd, pre-printed designs, cross-stitched, stenciled, colored, etc.

Iron. This is the process of flattening and smoothing a block or quilt with the aid of heat or steam using an electric iron. I recommend waiting until a block is completed to iron it.

Oncall Quilters. This group of very loyal quilters is available to me when I need people to make quilts or test directions or concepts. We meet on a regular basis to bounce ideas off each other. They are independent thinkers who love a challenge. There are also some Oncall Quilters outside the San Diego area. Quilters who have answered the call to make quilts for this book are definitely in my Oncall group.

Paper bag game. This is a fun way to select the colors or set for a quilt. I write the colors or adjectives for a color concept on separate slips of paper. I then put them into a brown paper bag, close my eyes and pick one from the bag. That becomes the color palette I am going to work with. The game concept can also be applied to the seven settings described in this book.

Sashing. These are strips of fabric used to separate blocks. The guideline for sashing strip width is one-fourth the size of the finished block. As an example, 10" finished blocks would use a $2^{1}/_{2}$" finished sashing strip.

Setting Map. Think of this like a blueprint. It is to be used as a guide, not something in concrete that must be followed exactly. Another name for Setting Map is Project Map, as seen in *Setting Solutions*.

Setting Triangles. Both side and corner triangles are necessary when you set your blocks on point, and together they are referred to as Setting Triangles. They straighten the edges of the quilt and can be plain, solid pieces of fabric, or pieced units to emphasize more design.

Size Reconciliation. When the blocks you are setting together into a quilt are different sizes, it is often necessary to make them all the same size before setting them together. I call this Size Reconciliation, which can be accomplished by remaking the blocks, trimming down the blocks, or adding to the blocks.

Stash. This is a valuable collection of fabric that is very important to most quilters.

Template. This is a pattern for a triangle, square, or other shape that is made from sturdy material and is used as a guide in cutting pieces for pieced blocks.

UFO. This term in quilting refers to an Un-Finished Object. Quilters often associate the term with blocks that aren't sewn into a quilt, a quilt in progress, or even a quilt top that is, as yet, not quilted or bound.

About the Author

You can visit Sharyn on her website at www.sharyncraig.com.

When Sharyn walked into the door of her first quilting class in the fall of 1978, she had no idea how that simple action would change the rest of her life. She had always loved to sew and do crafts. In fact she had been a Home Economics major in college, graduating with a degree in Clothing and Textiles. Just attending one quilting class made it clear what all that training had been leading up to.

Today she teaches, lectures, and writes about her passion, quiltmaking, and has authored twelve previous books. She has also been a regular contributor to *Traditional Quiltworks* magazine, having originated the Design Challenge column.

Going to the flannel wall and playing with the blocks is Sharyn's favorite aspect of making a quilt. She has always enjoyed figuring out how to set the blocks, what colors to use with them, and how to resolve the problems and challenges that those blocks present. She's frequently inspired by a quilt that she has already made and likes to use that same setting with a different set of blocks. She challenges herself to make this next quilt look different from the orig. She brings you this unique way of working with the blocks in this book.

Resources

Here are a couple of invaluable products that I recommend plus information on where you can order them if you can't find them at your local quilt shop.

Easy Center Square™ — This is a wonderful ruler if you need a square-on-point between 2" and 8". Designed by Sharon Hultgren, the ruler is available through your favorite quilt shop or *Connecting Threads* mail order at 800-574-6454.

John Flynn's Cut Your Own Template Kit — If you're a template person, I heartily recommend this product. It is a laminate product that is indestructible when using your rotary cutter. The kit comes complete with directions on how to use the material with the special cutter provided. For more information contact John Flynn at 800-745-3596 or visit his website at www.flynnquilt.com.

Other Books from C&T

For more information, ask for a free catalog:
C&T Publishing, Inc.
P.O. Box 1456, Lafayette, CA 94549
(800) 284-1114
Email: ctinfo@ctpub.com · Website: www.ctpub.com

For quilting supplies:
Cotton Patch Mail Order
3405 Hall Lane, Dept. CTB, Lafayette, CA 94549
(800) 835-4418, (925) 283-7883
Email: quiltusa@yahoo.com · Website: www.quiltusa.com

NOTE: Fabrics used in the quilts shown may not be currently available beause fabric manufacturers keep most fabrics in print for only a short time.

Index

* This quilt uses the Blue Star Block as its focus block.